The Gospel in Golf

Reflections on life
while playing a round of golf

John Horry

malcolm down

PUBLISHING

First published 2021 by Malcolm Down Publishing Ltd
www.malcolmdown.co.uk

24 23 22 21   7 6 5 4 3 2 1

British Library Cataloguing in Publication Data
A catalogue record for this book is available from the British Library.

ISBN 978-1-912863-87-7

Cover image © Dave Bate
Cover design and typesetting by Angela Selfe
Cartoon illustrations by Barry Diaper
Art direction by Sarah Grace

Images: (hole 10, 15 and 18) © Stephen Lee and used here with his permission. Image: of the author, page 143, ©Ste Park and used here with his permission. Image: of the Fellowship of the "Fore", page 17 © John Horry.

Trent Lock Golf Course overhead hole diagram graphics produced and supplied by Eagle. www.eagle.uk.com, Eagle Promotions Ltd maintains full copyright © 2021, used here with permission. Used also with the knowledge and permission of Trent Lock Golf and Country Club www.trentlockgolf.uk

Printed in the UK by Bell and Bain Ltd, Glasgow

For Pauline

my partner in life, who allows me to play golf.

"Few things draw men together more than a mutual inability to play golf."

P.G. Wodehouse

Contents

Foreword

Carl R. Trueman

John Horry and I have been friends now for nearly thirty years. It is a friendship built upon profound and irreconcilable differences and disagreements. I follow rugby while he is more of a football man. He supports Manchester City while if I had to choose a team from the "sport for stupid boys" as my headmaster influentially dubbed it, I would have to throw in my lot with Aston Villa. John is a Baptist, I am a Presbyterian. I am from the south of England while he is from the north. He was a high-flying captain of private industry, I am a teacher at an undergraduate college – and so, while we each regard ourselves as vital to civilisation, neither of us considers the other as having done a proper job or made a real contribution to the world. Above all, we disagree on golf. He is a passionate golfer whilst I regard as charitable understatement Mark Twain's famous dismissal of the game (I cannot bring myself to call it a sport) as a good walk spoiled.

And yet we do agree on a couple things. A good curry is the best meal. We each married up. And we both share a common Christian faith, believing that Jesus Christ of Nazareth was – and remains – God manifest in the flesh, and that he was born, lived, died, rose from the tomb, ascended, and will come again in power to save all those who have identified with him by faith.

For that reason, it is a pleasure to write this brief foreword to this book. Entertaining, concise and easy-to-read, it is the ideal book for the person who doesn't typically like books. It is also deceptively simple, for it manages to cover in a breezy, self-deprecating style the key elements of biblical teaching with regard to God, human beings, sin and salvation. The reader will be both entertained and edified.

Yes, John and I disagree on much. But our friendship holds firm after nearly three decades of such constructive conflicts, pursued as they always have been not only in the context of cordial banter and leg-pulling but also in the deeper soil of a shared Christian faith. Read this book, enjoy its humour, and ponder its message. It might be written by an incompetent golfer but it is still worth your while.

Carl R. Trueman
Grove City College
Pennsylvania

Foreword

Jason Griffiths

"A good walk spoiled" is a quip all golfers have thrown at them from time to time and one you learn to live with. Carl (the non-golfer) has already used it! Often as a golfer I find myself feeling sorry for the person and thinking they obviously don't see it as I do.

The same can be said for the Christian faith. As Christians we can sense others are looking at us thinking you just don't understand the world like I do. Or similarly, as Christians we can look at others thinking exactly the same thing!

What John does here is show us how he sees the world and loves golf, as a Christian. You may not agree with him; if you are just reading it for the golf anecdotes, I am sure you will completely understand and empathise. But one thing you need to know about John is that he is an encourager. I have lost count of the times I have played a bad shot and he has always managed to find a positive. "At least it has gone straight", "A good bad 'n'", "You missed the worst of the rough", "On the bright side it is not on the train tracks again" (see hole 7) etc., etc. He encourages not only in golf but also in life. I have known him now for over ten years, many of those playing golf. He is a leader in the church along with me and I am so thankful to God for him.

And if you can start to see how he sees the world from these chapters maybe he will encourage you to see that God is working in you and helping you to see he is there.

Jason Griffiths
Pastor, SBC, Stapleford,
Nottingham

Introduction

This small booklet is written for an esoteric[1] group of people. Sadly, for my purpose of getting rich (becoming a billionaire with my own Caribbean island and a wardrobe of mohair suits and electric boots[2]) – entirely the wrong group of people. These are the forgotten but heavily relied on few. Those who are constantly accused and rarely defended. Those who are characterised as bumbling, slightly idiotic and incompetent, simply never getting things right. Whereas the unspoken truth is that they are much loved, highly valued and greatly appreciated. These are those that rarely buy anything for themselves and no-one knows what to buy them for birthdays, Christmas or Father's Day. I am describing middle-aged (not to say "old"), golf-loving gentlemen and, to close the net even tighter, those that love their God and know Jesus as their Saviour. Yes, in a nutshell this is written for Christian, middle-aged, golf-playing men. If you only comply with one or even none of those descriptors, please read on though. If you have got this far you must have some interest in either the glorious gospel or the great game of golf.

Knowing their (those Christian, middle-aged, golf-playing men) short attention span, reading difficulties, and their tightly held belief that they never have enough time – I have kept it short.

In this book I will loosely draw an analogy between the Christian life and a round of golf. It is loose though, about

---

1. Look up the meaning of this word. You will discover it is the perfect noun for the group of people concerned. "Obscure", "mysterious", "cryptic".
2. Remember the song "Bennie and the Jets" by Elton John? You will if you are a man of a certain age. If not, ignore, and read on.

as loose as my 5-iron. The chances of me hitting any targets are extremely limited but, as I think every time I stand on the tee of the first hole, this may be my lucky (or blessed) moment. When on that tee I have simply three objectives in descending order of likelihood: (1) to have moved the ball in the right general direction; (2) to be able to see my ball again without searching; and (3) to be able to hit it a second time, roughly in the direction of the hole. So, standing here on the tee box of this book, three objectives: (1) to make you smile (a big task I know!); (2) to make you laugh; and (3) to encourage you to reflect on the goodness of God – the one who walks with us on the lifelong round. Often caddying, always encouraging and occasionally coaching by offering the necessary and massively valuable corrective advice.

Enjoy, and as I always tell myself before every outing with the clubs – don't take it too seriously; the serious things have already been dealt with.

John Horry FCIG[3]
Nottingham, April 2021

---

3. Fully certifiable incompetent golfer.

 Occasionally you will see a sign to the "next tee". At this point I recommend some further reading to build on the subject we have been "kind of" discussing during the playing of the hole. "Kind of" as in the sentence: "My second shot 'kind of' moved the ball in the direction of the green."

This is not meant to be a comprehensive review of Christian literature. Simply books I have recently read or which have been recommended to me. There is so much out there to help us! Books, online material including lectures, sermons, seminars, courses, etc. In fact, there is probably as much as there is on golf. The question for us is whether we are engaged enough to be truly interested in getting better. See more on this thought when you get to tee-off on hole 7.

The Players

This is a very brief description of some of the characters that get a mention as we play the round.

Phil – married to Gill, three grown children and a growing tribe of grandchildren. All-round good bloke, the social glue that holds us all together. His golf style can be described as "prudent". He also has a remarkable ability to hit trees in order to manoeuvre the ball to his advantage. In this respect I sense a divine blessing on his golf.

Jason – married to Catriona, three growing children. He is the pastor of the fellowship I belong to. As the youngest member of the "Holy" golfers and the only one working full-time (well, as a pastor – so "kind of" full-time), he gets out less than the rest of us. Always exciting when Jason is around, he has a genius for shaping his drives in circles and on one celebrated occasion took his own trolley out with his back-swing. There was shattered plastic everywhere!

Brian – married to Theresa. Four children and fostered five more.[4] Famous for his stylish headgear (reminiscent of the French Foreign Legion). He has many gadgets and aids to help him round the course, every shot being an exercise in science. His nickname is "Quiet Brian"; however, he is the sort of guy that when he does speak it is very well worth listening to.

---

4.   Wow! You have to say "wow". Nine children. No wonder Brian plays golf.

John (me) – married to Pauline, three grown children. At the time of writing, no grandchildren, but who knows about the moment that you are reading this?[5] Pretty much the weakest player, but I have my moments. Always one good shot a round that keeps me believing next time will be better. Lots of encouragement from my family. My youngest – when observing me putting – put his finger on the problem when he stated: "Dad, your putting would improve a lot if you got the ball closer to the hole!"

All of us have walked the Christian life for quite a while now and we can testify to the keeping and persevering nature of God. The one who knows all about us. He knows all about: our poor rounds, variable driving, dodgy irons, hopeless chipping and inept putting yet, despite that, he is the God who could not love us more.

The threesome ahead of us

Tony – an octogenarian. Spent his career as a quality manager for Rolls-Royce engineering and as a result has high standards for us all to maintain – especially in the wardrobe department. He, on occasions, recognises the effect of creeping age. He says, "I find it much more difficult to get out of bunkers these days. That is, after I have hit the ball!"

John S – top guy, salt of the earth. He knows how things are. His wit on the course is razor sharp. Always a great companion as we thwack our way around. Has a remarkable

---

5. Remarkably enough now I am proof reading the text I have had some delightful news. I am soon to be a grandfather!

tactic during match-play. He will describe, in eloquent and mouth-watering detail, what he had for Sunday lunch. This is amazingly successful. His opponents seem to find concentrating on their golf difficult with rumbling stomachs and pleasantly distracted minds.

John W – the man who knows the rules. If ever we have a dispute, we call John W in! If he does not know he will make it up. Extremely helpful chap. Famous for the electric trolley incident which will be described later, so keep reading. John is a great person to have around. In biblical terms he is the Barnabas, a constant encourager. He often says to me, "That was *almost* a good shot," which I think I am meant to take as encouragement.

The Fellowship of the "Fore" ready for action. From left to right. John (me), Jason, Brian and Phil. *Jason is from Grimsby so immune to sensing the cold, hence, the T-shirt.*

Hole 1

Fellowship of the "Fore"

On a gloriously mellow autumnal day we high-handicap golfers bumble around the first tee, with the self-contained delusion that today would be a good golfing day. After our polite and usual greetings, the impolite and humorous banter begins. Gentle teasing about the number of balls required for the round and how many wee stops will be necessary (men of a certain age!), that latest present received or an individual's choice of clothing is a rich vein of fun. Today Phil is wearing a pink ensemble which will live long in the memory. I liken its effect to a giant strawberry ice-cream. Jason mutters, so all can hear, something about a "marshmallow on legs".

Hole 1 at Trent Lock (see map) is the longest on the course: a 565-yard par 5. Why the course designers (those evil-minded men sitting in arm-chairs stroking white cats) put the longest hole first remains, to my mind, a constant cruelty. Old bodies that slowly warm up and easily wear out could do without having to hit three long and straight shots in succession as the first act of a 4-hour marathon. So, the usual scenario: Phil, the 3-times-a-week man, hits his drive down the middle but complains about the bad bounce that limits his "run on". Jason then takes aim. This is the moment of lottery. What happens next could be anything from 6 feet to 300 yards. We are all ready to scream with all the lung power we can muster "fore left" or "fore right". What happens is closer to the 6 feet than the 300 yards

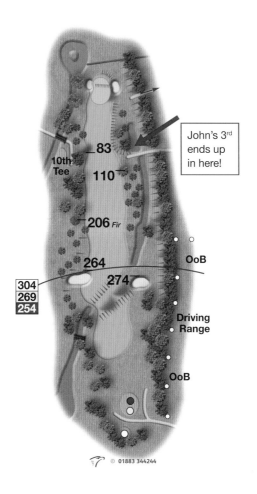

John's 3rd ends up in here!

10th Tee

83

110

206 Fir

264

274

304
269
254

OoB

Driving Range

OoB

© 01883 344244

and sadly there is no screaming required. Brian hits his standard tracer bullet of a drive straight into the little ditch carefully positioned on the left of the fairway. Finally, I slice my shot into the driving range that runs down the right. "One for Eddie,"[6] shouts Phil. I have grace[7] and manage to keep my second attempt somewhere on the fairway.

6. Eddie is the owner/manager of the course. So, balls lost to the range become his property and useful to him.
7. Our name for the "Mulligan". Refer to hole 5 for further explanation.

As we set off, I ask the question, "Is God good?" to which all my companions answer, "Yes."

"Is he good when the sun shines?"
"Yes."

"When the rain falls?"
"Yes."

"When I hit a good shot?"
"Yes."

"When I hook it straight into the rough?"
"Especially then," they say in unison with an unnecessary level of enthusiasm.

Hole 1 is always a struggle and again our scores demonstrate that. I make a complete mess of my third and end up losing a ball in the water to the right as we approach the green. Jason and Brian fare no better. Phil, the man in the pink, wins the hole scoring 7, holing a decent-length putt. The only two bits of good news are, firstly, we don't have to do hole 1 again and, secondly, Phil and I go 1 up.

Golf can be played alone but it is so much better to share. Sounds like the Christian life? Or life in general? Forget the nonsense of the ball and attempting to get it from tee to green using equipment specifically designed to make that difficult! I have found that men communicate better on a golf course than in a sharing meeting. Golf is second to eating as the perfect social activity. The way we play, competition is gentle,[8] and the truth is we are all willing each other on to succeed. We wish for putts to drop and

---

8. We generally have a four-ball match play. Jason and Brian vs Phil and John. We have honestly lost count but we must be closing in on 20 wins each. It has been going on for some time! At the time of this round, though, it had been a while since Phil and I had managed a win.

drives to go straight. Encouraging one another as we all know how it feels when it is not going well. We also know it is worth persevering because the playing and playing together is better than not bothering.

Keeping on, keeping on. The writer to the Hebrews knew a little about this. I doubt he played golf, but he knew about the Fellowship of the "Fore". To encourage each other, to walk with each other, to pray with and for each other even and especially when things are not going well.[9] The Christian life is to be walked together, in fellowship with each other and with God. God is good even when the shot is a huge hook or a staggering slice and all four of us are shouting "fore" until our throats are sore.

---

9. Hebrews 10:23-24.

	Hole 1
Par	5
SI	10
Phil (26)	7
SF	1
John (28)	8
SF	1
Jason (28)	8
SF	1
Brian (26)	8
SF	0

Match Play:
Phil and John
1 UP

Notes: *The number in parentheses is the player's handicap. The lower the better. 28 is the highest you, traditionally, could have* so this is an indication of our general level of incompetence. SF = Stableford. It is a scoring mechanism that allows for the handicap. Waste of time for us really but Jason and I (John) get 2 strokes on Phil and Brian. So, it feels important to me!*

*I am aware that modern handicapping systems allow higher numbers and I have applied for one.

Hole 2

Rules of the Game

Having endured the masochistic pleasure of hole 1 we walk along a small path to find the second tee. Despite the scoring system being agreed at the start of the round, the walk to the second tee is always the time to ensure we have an accord on the matter. We generally have at least three systems on the go. Stroke play, match play and Stableford. As you will understand when we get to hole 18, this multiplicity of scoring can give each of us a reason for being pleased. This brings me neatly to the subject of "Rules".

In concept, golf is beautifully simple: count the number of strokes from tee to hole. The lower the better. The principles are equally clear – the game is to be enjoyed and played in the right spirit. To quote the official rules:[10]

- Play the course as you find it and play the ball as it lies.

- Play by the rules and in the spirit of the game.

- You are responsible for applying your own penalties.

Honesty, integrity and having the right spirit are essential. The above is covered in one small section at the beginning of the rules. Yet the complete rules of golf extend to 240 pages, 24 sections and 70 definitions. How can something so simple become so complex? Answer: the need to have agreement and clarity across the community of golf as to how those beautifully simple principles are to be applied.

---

10. Rules of Golf, effective January 2019, R&A and USGA.

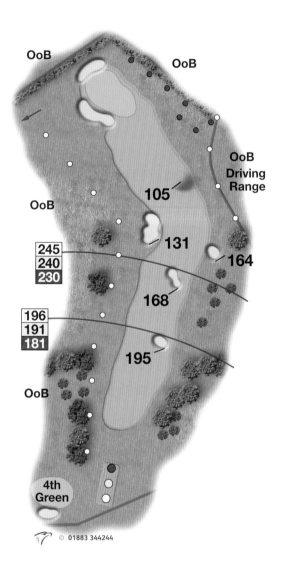

OoB

OoB

OoB
Driving
Range

105

OoB

131

245
240
230

164

168

196
191
181

195

OoB

4th
Green

© 01883 344244

Hole 2 is my least favourite hole on the course. It is a 420-yard, par 4, dog-leg left. It is rule bound due to its proximity to hole 3, the driving range and drainage ditches. There are:

- White posts down the left

- Red posts ahead.

- The fence at the back of the driving range is on the right as you come around the dog-leg (this is a useful position for hitting a wedge into the green).

It seems (according to those rules) if you hit your ball past the white posts you must take a penalty and replay the ball from its original position. Which always seems slightly mad to me. The white posts are there to protect players walking down the parallel fairway. This rule gives me a second go at taking someone out!

Pass the red posts and you must take a penalty but from the place where the ball passed the red post.

Hit the fence and you don't have to take a penalty and you can drop the ball for free, giving yourself a great opportunity to reach the green.

Can you understand the logic of that? For me there is an equal possibility of all three outcomes, stemming from the same high level of incompetence. Yet the consequences vary from "disaster" to "really quite helpful".

Approaching the green, we have great fun debating if the hole on the ground, that Jason's ball has rolled on, is an animal scraping or is of human origin. The rules of golf take the Christian creation view that the term "animal" does not include humans. If the scraping is of animal origin, then free relief (the ball can be moved without penalty) can be given. If of human origin then no relief is allowed.

We often share the same jokes. One of my favourites is the story of the golfer who accidentally strikes a passing

walker.[11] The ball hits the walker hard on the head rendering him unconscious. As luck (or the law of physics) dictates, the ball, after being deflected upwards off the walker's head, comes to rest on the unfortunate's face, fitting snuggly above his left eye. The golfer is understandably shocked. Having run over to the stricken walker he turns to his playing partner and with panic in his voice asks, "What do we do now?" His partner thinks for a moment and says, "Well don't think you are getting a free drop, you'll have to play the ball as it lies."[12]

We all know the game would be no fun at all without its principles and its systems (call that "law" or the "rules"). The rules are there to enable the game; without them it would be chaos and not golf. Yet the game can be spoiled and its spirit denied by an overzealous application of those rules. There is the Pharisaic spirit in each one of us that wants to judge others and their actions and attitudes on the golf course, yet we struggle to apply those same standards consistently to ourselves.

The laws of life are similar. A God-created world is best enjoyed when we live by the designer's principles. Jesus knew that but he also knew something about that Pharisaic spirit and the damage it can do.[13] Just like golf, *if* we take the course as we find it, play the ball as it lies, take responsibility for ourselves and apply the golden rule[14] – you never know – we may end up enjoying it and having a good round.

---

11. Strangely "walkers" are allowed on most golf courses. I am a little surprised health and safety risk assessments have not put an end to that. Perhaps we (golfers) need to improve our accuracy?
12. The partner is incorrect. Rule 11.1: "Ball in motion accidentally hits person or outside influence" would allow free relief in the situation described. There would be no reason to take a divot out of the unfortunate's head!
13. John 8:6-7.
14. Matthew 22:37-38.

	Hole 2	Total
Par	4	
SI	8	
Phil (26)	6	13
SF	2	3
John (28)	5	13
SF	3	4
Jason (28)	6	14
SF	2	3
Brian (26)	5	13
SF	3	3

Match Play:

Phil and John remain 1 UP

In terms of the golf, we all play it reasonably well. Brian is nearly perfect, just missing a par putt. I hole a decent-length putt to halve the hole. Phil and Jason do well to make a 6 after both finding the greenside bunker.

The evolution of our culture and morality is a very interesting topic. Where do the rules come from? The most insightful book I have read on this subject is **The Rise and Triumph of the Modern Self by Carl R. Trueman** (published by Crossway).

It is a shame that Carl, with that planet-like brain of his, cannot understand the beauty of golf. I am sure his lectures could be spiced up with no end of golfing wit and wisdom!

21st-Century Golfing Man

With hole 2 complete and some Stableford points in the bag we walk across to the tee box for hole 3. One member of our happy band has done well to last this far but he needs to nip behind the strategically placed bush. We are thankful that the course designers have been very sympathetic to the needs of the more mature gentleman. Our conversation often includes observations about our physical and mental deterioration. The ability to count is high on the list! A very useful ailment for a high-handicap golfer.

For some unknown reason, probably related to oncoming senility, a tune I used to know comes into my mind . . . "21st-Century Schizoid Man". I can remember nothing more than that line. None of my playing companions are able to help my failing memory. They clearly had a poor prog-rock education. So, Google to the rescue.[15] It is a King Crimson number. Like a lot of progressive rock lyrics, it is not altogether transparent in its meaning, but it seems like it is deep and meaningful. It is dystopian, for sure, looking forward to a depressing human future. It references concepts as bizarre as cat's feet, iron claws, neurosurgeons and paranoia's poison door.

With the rediscovered lyric rolling in my brain, I tee-off. Hole 3 is a short (131-yard par 3). Bunker to the right of me, bunker to the left, green to the front of me.[16] Beyond the bunkers on both sides there is what we call "cabbage"

---

15. Some players use mobile phone apps to help their golf. Distance finding or scoring. I only ever use it to support my failing memory.
16. Apologies to Alfred, Lord Tennyson.

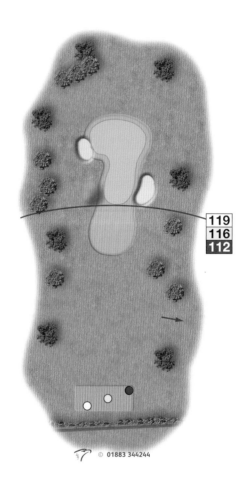

© 01883 344244

which is our code for heavy rough or what, in the UK, we call places of natural interest – which means nobody bothers mowing or cutting anything down. I push my shot slightly right, mercifully avoiding the cabbage and finding the bunker. My colleagues follow suit, two in the cabbage and one more in a bunker. My three companions all looked for excuses: "a fly alighted on the ball at the point of impact" – Brian; "I expected the wind to do a little more"

– Phil; and a new one from Jason – "there was a strange shiver up my leg just as I swung the club". From that point play improves with all four of us getting down with 3 more shots.

The threesome ahead of us (John S, John W and Tony) are half-way down the fourth fairway but have the time to make derogatory comments on our progress and to laugh again about Phil's marshmallow outfit. Tony is an octogenarian. Over lunch one day he shared with me how privileged he was to recently play a round of golf with his son and grandson. He was proud to say he lost. My question is, trying to bring the random thoughts of this chapter together, do we realise how blessed we are? Tony commented that this is probably the first time in human history (to make it sound dramatic) that three generations of "normal" people (not royalty or exceptionally rich) could play a game like golf together.

So, with our diminishing capabilities let's also recognise how blessed we are. The 21st-century golfing man. I try to make up a new version of the King Crimson lyrics. Needless to say, my three colleagues think I have lost the plot mumbling away to myself with "21st-Century Golfing Man" occasionally being shouted out at top volume. This is as good as it got:

Long life, pension draw,
Private healthcare screams for more
At longevity's pleasant door
21st-Century Golfing Man[17]

---

17. Apologies to King Crimson

In making this point I am aware that during my lifetime some of the most horrendous atrocities in human history have taken place. The killing fields of Cambodia, wars too numerous to list, famine on an industrial scale, persecution of minority races and religious beliefs. However, for a very normal British-born individual – of all the centuries of human history and all the centuries of Christian faith, this one is probably the best to date. Further, living in the developed West in the 21st-century is a massive privilege we should not underestimate. As a Christian I always believe that in God's kingdom the best is yet to come. We 21st-century golfing men have time, health and wealth to enjoy golf. We have, therefore, the time, health and wealth to serve in the growth of his kingdom by endeavouring to live useful, helpful, servant-hearted lives to benefit our fellow humans and to bring glory to our God.[18] Retirement[19] is not on offer in God's kingdom. He has a place and purpose for each one of us. I am also sure that a little more salt and light would work wonders in most golf clubs around the world.

---

18. Matthew 5:13-16. See also hole 11.
19. When my children were growing up and my mother-in-law was on childcare duty I often reminded her that the only reason God had granted her a long and healthy life was so she could help me out! A comment, as you can imagine, that was not always charitably received.

	Hole 3	Total
Par	3	
SI	16	
Phil (26)	4	17
SF	2	5
John (28)	4	17
SF	2	6
Jason (28)	4	18
SF	2	5
Brian (26)	4	17
SF	2	5

Match Play:

Phil and John remain 1 UP

The concept of "no retirement" in the Christian walk is not new. 21st-century golfing men and women have and will continue to have a huge role to play. Go and have a read of **Retired and Inspired by Wendy Billington** (published by the Bible Reading Fellowship).

The Devil's Green

The use of the apostrophe in the English language is always a source of good discussion and confusion. My sister, as a literary expert, could speak for hours on the subject. I won't do that. However, I will be clear on the name for this hole. "The Devil's Green" is intended to convey that the green on hole 4 is owned or perhaps designed by the ultimate evil. It is not intended to imply that I have some insight into the devil's skin colour or a comment on the fact that he is envious about something or other.

Flushed with our success on hole 3 (2 points each) we skip – metaphorically; literally, walk slowly – over to the tee box for hole 4. Hole 4 is a 372-yard, par 4, dog-leg right. There is a lake on the left (see map) in a perfect position for catching a well-struck but directionally challenged drive. Over to the right is a cabbage patch and a bunker. Once at the apex of the fairway things get reasonably simple, that is if you avoid the small bunkers on the left and right of the green. Simple that is, until . . . (cue the *Jaws* music) . . . you are on the Devil's Green.

Phil goes straight, twice, and ends up in front of the green in two. Jason goes bendy, twice, but still can hit the green with his third. Brian clatters a tree with his second and is in the cabbage. I, remarkably, follow Phil's example but get slightly closer to the edge of the green with my second. Then the fun begins . . . (cue the *Jaws* music) . . . on the Devil's Green.

The green is like a scale model of the Yorkshire Moors with undulations a plenty. It is inevitable that on such a

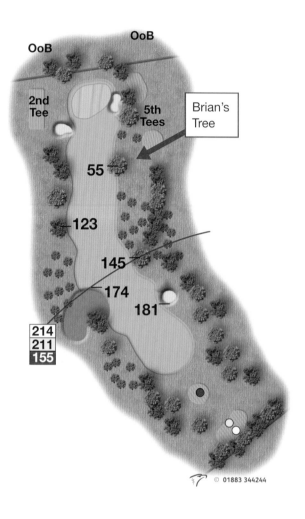

green there are valleys and troughs where gravity will pull a spherical object. Like the famous final day 16th pin position at Augusta where 9 hole-in-ones have been made in the last 10 years. This is primarily due to the green keeper's decision to position the pin in a valley.[20] On the Devil's Green

---

20. Watch the YouTube clip of Matt Kuchar's hole-in-one from April 2017.

at Trent Lock the pin is *never* positioned in a valley. It is always at the summit or, even worse, on a slope. This leads me to wonder if the green keepers have had special training or undergone a delicate "compassion bypass" operation to be able to continuously inflict this cruelty. Where is their love? Where is their kindness? Where is their goodness? Where is their gentleness? Where is their self-control?[21]

(In fact, I am severely tempted, at this point, to personify the green keepers as evil but that would take an illustration too far and be grossly unfair. The picture of the devil riding around on his mowing machine trying to lay traps and temptations for the unsuspecting golfer does have its biblical parallels – but I am sure you will agree, as an illustration it carries many dangers and potential misunderstandings – best not go there!)

Brian chips out of the cabbage and with a level of physics-defying wonder, rolls up the slope to stop pin high. Jason plays next. A good shot climbing the summit, hanging for a brief and tense moment before disappearing down the slope to end a good 12 feet away. Phil attacks the flag; the ball grips the slope and veers right to give a symmetry to the layout being 12 feet away but opposite Jason's. Finally, I take my putter, fearing that I might follow Jason over the top, I under-hit the putt and fail to get up the slope before the ball slides back down. I won't bore you with more of the details but just to record that Brian manages a par, it takes Phil and Jason 2 more and me another 3 – gosh, I hate that green with undiminishing passion!

---

21. I did try to get all the fruit of the Spirit (Galatians 5:22-23) in at this point but could not see the relevance of joy, peace, patience or faithfulness to the groundsmen and the positioning of holes.

So, having avoided the temptation to pin evil on the groundsmen,[22] instead I will draw the analogy between the green and human nature – however much we try to play it straight and true, there is an inherent bias in our nature. The Apostle Paul described it well.[23] Like the undulating green – it seems to be how we are. Our attitudes, actions and affections often seem to make us fall and slip down the slope. Wherever your theology takes you. Whether Augustinian or Pelagian, whether original sin, sins of commission or sins of omission – we all must recognise we are far from flawless. If pictured as a green, our nature is undulating and not the perfect surface we would like to think it is or, more importantly, as God requires it to be.

The Bible is crystal clear that we have a problem. Romans 3:23. The word "sinner" is a description of an arrow that fails to fly to its target. In a golfing scenario we can[24] see the reason on the Devil's Green, hole 4. That reason is to do with fallen human nature that affects us all. With that rather depressing thought, let's move on to hole 5 where things get significantly better.

---

22. For the record – the groundsmen/green keepers are a fabulous bunch and do a great job.
23. Romans 7:21-24.
24. "All have sinned and fall short of the glory of God" (Romans 3:23).

	Hole 4	Total
Par	4	
SI	2	
Phil (26)	5	22
SF	3	8
John (28)	6	23
SF	2	8
Jason (28)	5	23
SF	3	8
Brian (26)	4	21
SF	4	9

Match Play:

ALL SQUARE

Brian achieves a very impressive par to win the hole. This after clattering into a tree with his second but his third brilliantly rescues the situation.

Hole 5

G is for the God

With three of us reeling from our experience on the Devil's Green, we wander over to the 5th. One of the easier holes on the course (stroke index 14). A 327-yard, par 4 with a gentle left-hand bend on the fairway. The standard mantra is to stay right and you'll likely get a shot in. Go left and you're in somewhat of a pickle. The ball will nestle down nicely in the small patch of cabbage with a tree or two between you and the green. Go a long way left and the threesome ahead (remember them? John S, John W, and Tony) are in danger on the 6th fairway. *(However, at the point of us arriving on the 5th tee none of the threesome can be seen. Phil comments, "They have all nipped behind the bush." Sure enough, one by one, they all re-emerge, now relieved, to continue their progress.)*

Once off the tee and down the right side of the fairway there is little to worry about other than two bunkers positioned to the left and right of the green. Immediately left of the tee box is a thick hedge, presumably positioned to protect those on the 6th green from a dramatically pulled tee shot.

Off we go – Brian, Phil and I all manage to get down the fairway. Jason, as already noted, has an incredible ability to shape the ball in a left to right circle. If the shot was straight, I maintain my view he would be one of the longest hitters in the game. Jason takes aim and we all hold our collective breath. It is another special, flying off at great pace to the left. Sadly, though, this one does not have the opportunity to turn right as it embeds itself, accompanied by the

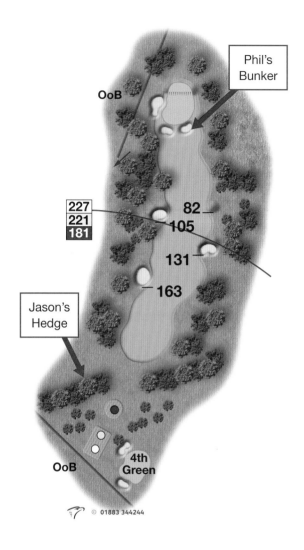

Phil's
Bunker

OoB

227
221
181

82
105

131

163

Jason's
Hedge

OoB

4th
Green

© 01883 344244

sound of cracking twigs and thorns, in the above-mentioned thick hedge (the course map should help explain the resultant situation).

We all look at each other feeling Jason's pain and utter the word "Grace". Grace is our term for what other golfers call the "Mulligan". The rules insist that Jason should either hack the ball out of the hedge or take a drop two club lengths from the hazard, which in this case does not give much chance for progress down the fairway. Grace means that Jason gets a second shot off the tee. The score will not reflect the first shot. It will simply be forgotten. Just as if it never happened.

Grace is beautiful and fundamental to an understanding of the Christian faith. I won't try to press golfing analogies any further but leave it to God's Word. Let's read Ephesians 2:4-5:

> *"But because of his great love for us, God, who is rich in mercy, made us alive with Christ even when we were dead in transgressions – it is by grace you have been saved."*

Or try the continuation of the verse I referenced on hole 4 – Romans 3:23-24:

> *"For all have sinned and fall short of the glory of God, and all are justified freely by his grace through the redemption that came by Christ Jesus."*

Just like when you are on a golf course and you breathe and take in the beauty of the surroundings and praise God for his physical creation. At this point in your reading, just breathe. Take a moment and try (you will never succeed) to take in how much God has loved you. Praise God for his spiritual re-creation – because of grace alone, through the work of Christ alone, by faith alone.[25]

---

25. You may recognise these as three of the five solas of the Protestant Reformation and are central to the theology of salvation. The other two are through scripture alone and to the glory of God alone.

We sing with our kids at church about GRACE.

G is for the God who poured his love upon us
R is for the rebels we all turned out to be
A is his amazing love which none of us deserve
C is for Christ Jesus who gave his life for me
E is for ever, forever more his love will never end[26]

Back to the golf. Remember my description of the hole? Once on the fairway, little more to worry about other than two bunkers left and right guarding the mouth of the green. By golfing grace Jason has joined us on the fairway. Brian and I take our second shots and get close to the green; both of us end up down in 5. Jason hits a "peach" (a term for a good shot – he does not hit a piece of fruit – that would make quite a mess!) and now has a very rare thing for us – a putt for a birdie. Phil, in the best position from his first shot hits another "peach". The ball is flying straight for the gap between those bunkers but then **disaster**. The ball must hit a small stone or a twig and violently bounces right and is swallowed by the right-hand bunker. Feeling victimised and aggrieved by this unfortunate turn of events, with a frown on his Yorkshire face Phil exclaims: "Grace abounds but there is no justice!"[27]

---

26. Despite searching the internet, I cannot find the authorship of these words. It is one of those songs we simply keep singing.
27. Justice = getting what we deserve. Mercy = not getting what we deserve. Grace = getting what we do not deserve. In this case, Phil clearly believed his shot deserved better than the bunker. More to be said on this – keep reading.

	Hole 5	Total
Par	4	
SI	14	
Phil (26)	4	26
SF	3	11
John (28)	5	28
SF	2	10
Jason (28)	4	27
SF	3	11
Brian (26)	5	26
SF	2	11

Match Play:

ALL SQUARE

Justice is (kind of) achieved as Phil manages a neat bunker escape and Jason misses his birdie putt. No-one, at this stage, reminds Jason of the "grace" he had received. Come hole 12 (read on) I may mutter it in my distress.

My son's mother-in-law has recommended that he, annually, should read **What's So Amazing About Grace? by Philip Yancey** (published by Zondervan). A classic. *It is an interesting recommendation from a mother-in-law.*

Grace is a truly stunning and beautiful biblical concept. For a fuller understanding of it and its context within reformation history can I recommend **Grace Alone by Carl R. Trueman** (published by Zondervan).

The Narrow Way

At 215-yards, hole 6 is a long par 3 (for golfers of our incompetence). It is quite simply straight. A narrow fairway. A few bunkers (which in my experience rarely come into play – perhaps if we were better, they would), but on the right is a boundary hedge (no hope if you slice over or into there), and on the left is the dreaded cabbage. The hedge and the cabbage often come into play. The only sensible way is straight down the middle.

On the 5th Jason, sadly, missed his birdie putt; this combined with Phil's equally impressive par (following a neat bunker escape) shortened Phil's chuntering about injustice. Jason has the honour and tees-off. He seems unable to hit a straight drive, again the ball is sent on a circular sight-seeing tour. It takes in views of the 5th fairway, the cabbage and trees before landing, like a guided drone, in the middle of the fairway a few yards short of the green. Brian hits long but slices and ends up rolling into the base of the right-hand hedge. Phil goes straight but someway short of Jason. I go straight but in the wrong direction. A beautiful connection but simply the wrong line. The ball flies majestically but left, clearing the cabbage and scurrying across the 5th fairway to come to rest a long way wide.

At this point we part company. I wander off to find my errant ball while Phil helps Brian excavate the hedge bottom in search of the second missing-in-action ball. Both searches are successful.

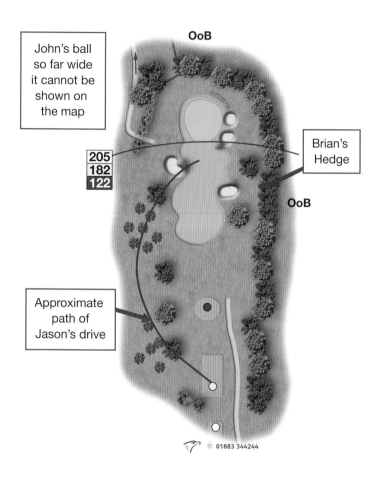

OoB

John's ball
so far wide
it cannot be
shown on
the map

Brian's
Hedge

205
182
122

OoB

Approximate
path of
Jason's drive

© 01883 344244

I must reflect, while trying hard to chip my ball onto the green and observing Brian removing thorns from his trousers after his hedge excavation, that it would have been so much easier and, potentially, more enjoyable, if we had hit the ball straight.

Jesus talks about a "narrow way".[28] Modern society seems to want to reject this idea but when you observe all the "rough" that we seem to find ourselves in we must

---

28. Matthew 7:13-14.

conclude, on occasions, that simply following the "narrow way" would have made the whole thing so much easier and more enjoyable.

It is a very real dilemma for the 21st-century golfing man – how to keep the ball straight and avoid the rough and the sand-traps.[29] It is also a huge dilemma for the Christian church – how to follow the "narrow way" without becoming judgemental in our attitudes and actions. Such attitudes and actions often land us in the accusatory sand-traps that we would have done so much better to avoid.

This is clearly getting serious now and somewhat removed from the jolly round of golf you were expecting. So, I won't explore it much more here. I would add, though, that there are no "isms" or "phobias" in true Christianity. In Christ there is no male or female, Greek or Jew, rich or poor, slave or free. All are welcomed into the kingdom, and God sent his son for them. Around the throne in heaven, the golf player will be there alongside the dog-walker![30] However, in living the Christian life there is the "narrow way". To be narrow is sometimes very helpful and sensible. My car runs on diesel. Very restrictive? It won't run on petrol, fine wine, or even Phil's best single malt. So it is with Christian living, we should look at what is fuelling it. What we watch and read and the conversations we have. How we behave and the attitudes and thoughts we nurture. If you want to lower your golf score, then work on hitting the ball straight. If you want to be a more effective witness for him, then work on staying on the narrow way. We will also find it is far more fun and satisfying. Just like making a par 3 on hole 6 compared with the 5 I ended up with – if only I had gone straight down the middle!

---

29. "A sand-trap is a deep depression of sand, filled with golfers in deep depressions," credited to Henry Beard in *A Little Bit of Golfing Wit* by Tom Hay (Summersdale, 2018).
30. Not quite how it is expressed in Revelation 7:9 but you get my drift.

	Hole 6	Total
Par	3	
SI	12	
Phil (26)	4	30
SF	2	13
John (28)	5	33
SF	1	11
Jason (28)	3	30
SF	3	14
Brian (26)	4	30
SF	2	13

Match Play:

Jason and Brian
1 UP

Jason follows up on his excellent drive and takes the hole. You may also notice that he takes the lead on the SF scoring!

***The Hole in Our Holiness* by Kevin Deyoung** (published by Crossway). How to live lives following Christ.

Continuous Improvement

We often try to help each other with our combined wisdom on the mechanics of the golf swing. I am not sure that our combined wisdom adds up to much though. We share thoughts about the "take-away" (not the Chinese from the night before) and the height/speed of the backswing. Acceleration on the downswing, angle of the club head at impact, the follow through and, most important of all, the turn and finish. Like a fine wine, the finish to a good golf swing is always smooth but complex. We all have slightly different interpretations on the turn and finish. I have taken to trying to point my left toe in the direction I want the ball to go. Phil leans hard over to the side he wants the ball to move to. Brain tends to run on the spot and Jason tightens his butt cheeks. After years of serious study, I have concluded that all the toe pointing, body leaning, on the spot jogging and buttock clenching makes absolutely no difference to the outcome. A golf ball has its own consciousness and will fly wherever it wants! I do think, on occasions, that the only difference between us and the golfers on the PGA Tour is that they have better golf balls that know golf better than the cheap ones we have to work with.

Well, of-course, that is total nonsense. A golf ball has a rubber core and is coated in plastic. It does not have consciousness.[31] The flight of the ball is determined by

---

31. A golf ball is made of a solid synthetic rubber core (polybutadiene) inside a durable thermoplastic (ionomer resin) cover. Between 300 and 600 has been shown to be the optimal number of dimples. As the ball spins the air movement around the dimples creates lift. So, in a sense the ball does fly!

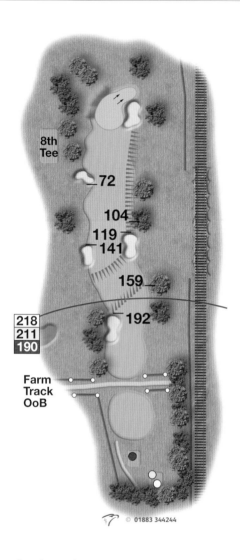

8th Tee

_72

104_

119 ─

─ 141

159_

218
211
190

─ 192

Farm
Track
OoB

© 01883 344244

Newtonian physics. There are many interesting (?) studies to be read about the number of dimples on a golf ball and their impact on flight, spin and control! If it was possible to take all variability out of the swing, environment, club face and ball condition then the outcome of each shot could be planned and implemented perfectly. As difficult as it is for me to accept – it is possible to get better and more consistent at golf. It is not the case that I am serially unlucky, the hard truth is: I am not good at playing golf. Although helpful to my mental health, no amount of blaming the ball can detract from my lack of true golfing talent.

Back to the round. Brian suggests that Jason shortens his backswing and holds the club for a few microseconds before letting it descend. The resulting shot is a drive rising and falling in perfect parabolic shape. "The professionals would charge you at least £25 for that, Jason," says Phil. Phil stands on the tee and you can hear the cogs of the brain turning, thinking through the mechanics from take-away through to finish. The result – a pulled shot that skips off left at a great rate. "Fore left," we scream (we note John W, now on the 8th, diving behind a tree for cover). Fortunately for Phil the 8th fairway comes to his rescue and his ball ends up in a good and playable position. Unfortunately for our entertainment purposes, he also misses John W! John's comments were very amusing, but not printable.

Hole 7 is a 384-yard par 4. Wonderfully simple. A tight fairway with a railway down the right. Engine drivers seem to delight in sounding their horn just as we are about to thwack the ball. Jason once got his own back by putting four balls on the track. Lots of grace required that day!

As we move off from the tee, we continue to discuss the whole concept of trying to understand our golf swing. I recollect the film *Tin Cup* starring Kevin Costner as Roy McAvoy. I remember the scene where Roy's caddie and coach (Romeo Pasar played by Cheech Marin) tries to get him to hit a decent shot on the range and tells him the following: "move the change from left to right pocket", "tie your left shoe lace in a double bow", "put your hat on backwards" and "place a tee behind the left ear". Roy McAvoy feeling angry and humiliated then hits the perfect iron. Romeo then tells him, "Your brain is getting in the way – just hit the ball!"

I proceed to "just hit the ball" and win the hole with a par – very nice too!

I have had a single golf lesson and looked at some videos on YouTube, but the truth of the matter is that I am honestly not too bothered about getting better. I love golf just as it is for me. It is serious enough for it to mean something but not enough for it to cross the line into importance. For four hours – tee to hole – it matters, and then after that, it does not.

As a bigger problem though, I think I have the same attitude to my Christian life. I am probably far too casual about it. Sitting here writing this I am being challenged and would like to challenge you. Are we serious about being better in the worship and service of our Lord? It is wonderfully true that Jesus loves and accepts us as we are. *"But God demonstrates his own love for us in this: while we were still sinners, Christ died for us"* (Romans 5:8). However, Jesus loves us far too much to leave us as we are. There is a progression and development in Christian living. We are to move from the "milk" to the "meat".[32]

Jason often reminds us (while doing his job as pastor – which, I hasten to add, he is better at than he is at golf) that "we have been saved", "we are being saved" and "we will be saved". God is working his purposes out in us; the process of sanctification is an ongoing work. We need to be willing "golfers" in his hands as he rebuilds our swing. Or as Ezekiel 36:26b expresses it, *"I will remove from you your*

---

32. Hebrews 5:11 – 6:1 and 1 Corinthians 3:1.

heart of stone and give you a heart of flesh." The objective is daily to be more like Jesus. Neither you nor I can do anything about the round of golf we played yesterday but we can learn for the next one. So it is in Christian living; yesterday is gone[33] but tomorrow we can ask for his help and apply ourselves to being more like Christ. Saint Francis of Assisi's prayer is appropriate at this point: *"These three things, dear Lord I pray. To see thee more clearly, follow thee more nearly, love thee more dearly. Day by day."*

I am considering getting a T-shirt printed – on the front it will read: "I will never get any better at golf", and on the back: "but still – I will end up in heaven."

---

33. Another 1970s song title in there somewhere!

	Hole 7	Total
Par	4	
SI	4	
Phil (26)	6	36
SF	2	15
John (28)	4	37
SF	4	15
Jason (28)	6	36
SF	2	16
Brian (26)	7	37
SF	1	14

Match Play:

back to
ALL SQUARE

I (John) am delighted with this outcome. If you are following the match play, you will note that winning this hole is my first real contribution.

Making good decisions as discussed during our thwack over holes 6 and 7 is further debated in a book by **Keith Gentry** entitled *Good Choices* (published by Malcolm Down Publishing). Worth a read.

Hole 8

Lost and Found

Hole 8 has the signature photo shot for the course. A green painted metal bridge over a small lake with a pleasant view across the parkland towards the river. Very pretty in the autumn with all those glorious colours. Not quite Augusta or South Conway, but all the same, not too bad. (I am sure if I was a member of Generation Y I would regularly share photos on Instagram or Facebook – but I am not – so I don't.)

Hole 8 is a 321-yard par 4, a sharp dog-leg right with a pitch over the above-mentioned bridge and lake onto the green.

We all tee-off. I play prudently with a 7-iron knowing I will need a second to put me in position for pitching over the water. Jason slaps his shot round the trees on the left, Brian goes smack up the middle and Phil, quite unusually, misses the water. All four of us in good position. This puts a skip in our communal stride as we set off down the fairway.

Half way down the 8th fairway is a primitive enclosure which is locally called a "toilet". It contains no porcelain, gold taps, hand sanitisers or warmed towels. In fact, nothing much that civilised people would expect to find in a facility so named. However, it serves a very useful purpose as now we are about 90 minutes into the round and bladders are beginning to strain! So, there is always a brief intermission in proceedings as the necessary occurs.[34]

---

34. I asked my daughter to act as my editor and she is really quite shocked that weeing is allowed on a golf course. She had the opinion they were posh and respectable places.

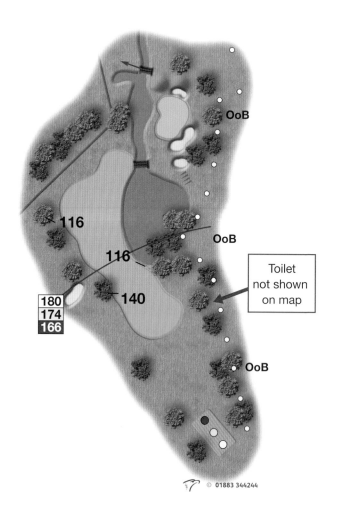

OoB

116

116

OoB

| Toilet |
| not shown |
| on map |

180
174
166

140

OoB

01883 344244

Phil hits his second shot pin-high onto the green (fantastic, much rejoicing), Jason drops his in the water (no rejoicing), Brian in the bunker and I slice mine into the rough over to the right of the green. It is going to be some time before Phil needs to play again so he regresses into his obsession of searching for lost golf balls. He has an innate ability to find and rescue them. Dressed in his marshmallow outfit, he enthusiastically sets about his task with his long ball retriever (a telescopic steel device with a cup on the end). As we (Jason, Brian and I) set about trying to avoid dropping too many shots, we hear shouts of glee: "Callaway ERC Soft", "Titleist Pro V1" and "It's a MacGregor!" He approaches the green with a handful of finds. Throwing an old Dunlop at me saying, "It is not very good; would you like it?"

I note that many golfers mark their golf balls with initials or symmetrical markings to help their putting. I can't think, though, I have ever seen a happy smiley face on a golf ball. Given we are very soon to lose them we probably don't want the emotional trauma that would occur if we got too attached. Consequently, we tend not to give them faces or names or talk to them kindly. I must ask at this point (seriously slowdown in your reading and consider carefully), have we ever thought about this from the ball's point of view? They are smacked around, shouted at for not going in the right direction, slung angrily into bags and generally not appreciated for being round and perfectly dimpled! Then on hole 8 when the careless golfer slaps them into the water or the bushes they are simply and uncaringly left out in the wet and the cold – lost, helpless and hopeless, no longer able to fulfil their purpose for existing. Then Philip (the golf ball saviour) appears. Although he has a bag full of balls, he will leave those to search out and rescue the lost. You can hear the Titleist Callaway choir singing his praises.

Jesus didn't include a golf ball in his trilogy of lost things (sheep, coin, son)[35] but the sense is the same. It is very clear, in fact central to the message of the gospel, that Jesus was

35. Luke 15

sent by his heavenly Father on a seek and save mission.[36] Jesus said it himself very clearly.[37] He also demonstrated it. He often walked off the fairway and joined people in the rough of life. For example, he met with "tax collectors and sinners",[38] famously travelled out of his way for a conversation with the Samaritan woman[39] and he reached out, touched and healed the leper.[40] His whole mission is summed up in Philippians 2:6-11: the one who stepped out of heaven on his seek-and-save mission that took him all the way to the cross.

Jason and I have both used the illustration of the wayward golf ball and the golfer who goes out of his way to retrieve it in our children's talks at church or in school assemblies. Waving the long telescopic device around always brings a laugh. We all like sheep (or golf balls?) have gone astray.[41] This life can be hard. We can be slapped about, blamed (rightly and wrongly), not appreciated and often lose our way and end up in the rough, a bunker or, even worse, out of bounds. But the Son of Man came to seek and save that which was lost.[42] I, for one, am very glad he did.

---

36. John 3:16
37. Luke 19:10
38. Luke 15:1
39. John 4
40. Mark 1:40-45
41. Isaiah 53:6
42. Luke 19:10

	Hole 8	Total
Par	4	
SI	6	
Phil (26)	4	40
SF	4	19
John (28)	6	43
SF	2	17
Jason (28)	6	42
SF	2	18
Brian (26)	6	43
SF	2	16

Match Play:

Phil and John
go 1 UP

Phil was simply magnificent on this hole. Not only did he save many a golf ball but played the hole in regulation. Over the lake and onto the green in 2 followed by an excellent putt and a tap-in for par.

Try reading **The Search for God by Peter May** (published by Malcolm Down Publishing). A challenge to us to enthusiastically engage in reaching 21st-century people with a reasoned faith that answers those difficult questions.

May the Humming Never Stop

After his significant finds and quite excellent score from the previous hole Phil is, to say the least, jolly. He is humming a well-known Christmas carol (a little premature given we are still in autumn and many leaves are still on the trees). The carol is something called "Joy to the World". Jason makes the comment that "after a couple more holes the funeral march may be more appropriate". Such is the fickle and transient nature of our pleasure in the standard of our golf. Somewhat similar to what we do in life. Our mood shifts in accordance with the seemingly random events that come our way. "The slings and arrows of outrageous fortune."[43]

The Bible talks about "joy" or happiness as something that is not fickle, transitory or random. It speaks of something that is deep and permanent. The last section in the letter James wrote seems to be all about a relationship with God in both good and bad times. He speaks about happiness. The Greek word James used was *euthumei*. I am told by more scholarly men[44] that this splits into two. The preposition *eu* meaning "well" or "good". And then the verbal form of the noun *thumos* meaning "soul" (the centre of one's life and meaning). Putting this together then "happiness" as defined by James is: WELL-GOOD DEEP IN SOUL. Not a superficial euphoria[45] but a deep inner sense of well-being. This fixed joy comes from a living and loving

---

43. Shakespeare, *Hamlet*.
44. In this case John Blanchard from his commentary on James, *Truth for Life* (Evangelical Press, 2015).
45. Another Greek word with the same preposition but has become associated with transitory happiness.

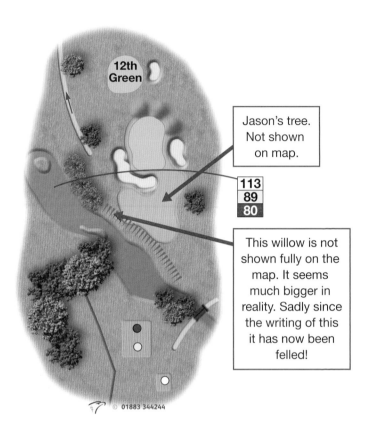

12th Green

Jason's tree. Not shown on map.

113
89
80

This willow is not shown fully on the map. It seems much bigger in reality. Sadly since the writing of this it has now been felled!

© 01883 344244

relationship with the Living and Loving God. It is something to be enjoyed irrespective of the quality of the next shot.

With this marvellous doctrine in mind and with Phil still humming "Joy to the World" we set about hole 9. Don't forget there is a gently competitive match ongoing that is heating up as the round proceeds. It's Jason and Brian versus Phil and John. Hole 9 is the shortest hole, a mere 100 yards. However, that 100 yards is over a lake, a bunker and an extremely large willow tree. To hit the green a pitching wedge needs to project the ball very high over all three hazards. As it is autumn time the tree is in desperate need of pruning. Its branches are spreading out over the green. This brings an entirely new form of entertainment into play. From the tee you have no view of the other side of the willow and a brilliantly struck shot destined for the hole can be caught and cruelly diverted by an unforgiving, overhanging branch. "To hit a branch or not to hit a branch, that is the question."[46]

I suspect you can guess what happens. Phil and I, with the honour, go first. Phil's shot is high and handsome but as it drops, we hear the noise of ball on timber. The ball must have bounced within the tree, between its branches. The next we hear of it is the sickening "plop" as it falls into the lake. I go next; again it is a beautiful shot, arching up and over the willow. Then that awful noise as it is caught by one of those overhanging branches and we see the ball fall, apologetically, into the greenside bunker. Phil and I, feeling extremely frustrated, comment philosophically, with a few well-chosen words[47] on the injustice of these events.

Then the opposition. Brian hooks his tee shot. It is destined to fall left of the green. Then the Whomping Willow[48] intervenes again. This time to divert the ball onto the green giving Brian one of those very rare birdie opportunities (which he later takes with aplomb). Jason hits a horrible shot. What's new? It travels at little more than head height wide and to the right of the willow. Incredibly it hits the base of a small, staked tree and deflects towards the green coming to rest on the fringe with a good view of the hole. Absolutely unbelievable!

---

46. Not quite Shakespeare but could have been if the Bard had played golf.
47. Well-chosen words that are, again, best not printed!
48. A Harry Potter reference for those that find that image helpful.

Upon leaving the tee Phil and I, both still chuntering about injustice, know that we have lost this hole. The humming has, not surprisingly, stopped. Jason wanders over to me and whispers, "It must be very hard for you two playing us three!"

I think I can conclude from other events that there is no divine intervention in favour of either team although Jason's comment had me giggling for quite some time. The joy in golf may be short-lived but our joy in our Lord is eternal and the humming need never stop. Jesus came that we might know what it is to be children of God[49] and we can live in the fullness and joy of that relationship.[50]

49. Romans 8:16: "The Spirit himself testifies with our spirit that we are God's children."
50. John 10:10: "I have come that they [you] may have life and have it to the full."

	Hole 9	Total
Par	3	
SI	18	
Phil (26)	5	45
SF	1	20
John (28)	5	48
SF	1	18
Jason (28)	4	46
SF	2	20
Brian (26)	2	45
SF	4	20

Match Play:

back to
ALL SQUARE

We are told that true joy is found in him. Try reading **Gentle and Lowly by Dane Ortlund** (published by Crossway). Looking to understand the heart of Jesus. You will find joy there.

Hole 10

From There to Here

As we are now half-way round, 9 holes done and 9 still to do, we take stock on the 10th tee. We often pass round chocolate bars (Jason always seems to find a two-for-one deal at the local convenience store). Phil and I have a nip of whisky[51] (or whiskey in my case, generally having the Irish form). On a cold day, it hits the spot! "Good job something can hit a spot," I cannot help thinking. Our conversation has bounced from the sublime (chatting about God and Christian things) through to the ridiculous (today it has been Phil's marshmallow outfit that has prompted most commentary, which Phil takes in his gracious stride[52]).

The match situation is on a knife's edge as it normally is. It is all square with both teams having won 3 holes and halved the other 3. Tense stuff. Individual scores are not bad either. It is not often we reach the turn below 50 but on this occasion we all have.[53] I feel like I am playing quite well but I have the worst score of 48. Phil and Brian lead the way on 45 with Jason not far behind on 46. Hole 10 is a 370-yard, dog-leg right, par 4. The significant hazard is the lake between the end of the fairway and the green. (Lots of lakes on this course! I guess it is due to its proximity

---

51. Just an observation at this point: Scotland is the birth place of golf. It is not surprising, therefore, that it is the birth place of whisky.
52. Without doubt plotting his revenge. I would also note that after having read the proof of this book his wife claims to have thrown the offending garments away. So a photograph, to help entertain you, was not possible.
53. The professional golfers amongst you will take issue with this, given the liberal use of "grace" as explained in hole 5.

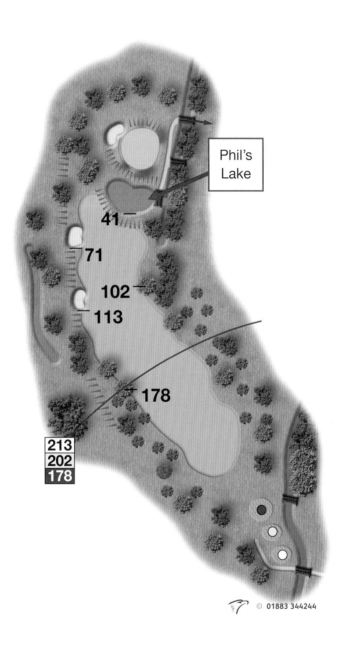

to the river and the associated canal system[54] – the 18th-century way of getting goods from "here to there".) The point of knocking the ball over the lake is the make-or-break point on the hole. Will the shot get over? Or will it go in the lake? Will we be successful in getting from "here (the fairway) to there (the green)"?

We all struggle a little to get in position taking 3 shots rather than the expected 2. Phil has got there via a bunker, Jason through the trees, Brian has fought his way across the parallel fairway (taking further verbal grief from John S, John W and Tony ahead of us). I have blocked off the tee not getting very far at all but thankfully two decent shots have got me alongside my playing partners.

Now the tense movie music starts as each one of us takes a 9-iron or pitching wedge to try and float the ball, McIlroy-like, over the lake and onto the green. The tense notes hang in the air. Jason first – well it's over but to the left of the green in a really inhospitable area of mud and ruts. Then Brian, lots of earth gets thrown up but the ball does not move very far. Not in the lake, but not over it either. Phil is a player who suffers from the dreadful golfing disease of hydrophobia.[55] The symptoms of the disease are obvious in the trembling of the knees and the apparent cessation of any ability to swing a club when within 50 yards of water. His groan can be heard in the clubhouse as the ball plops (a truly distressing sound) into the middle of the lake

---

54. Trent Lock is so named as it is the location of a lock on the River Trent. Locks were the height of Georgian civil engineering being the system by which canal boats can be lifted up or down the canal system. The area is a major canal navigation junction, where the River Soar and Erewash Canal meet the Trent and Mersey Canal by way of the River Trent and the adjacent Cranfleet Cut. It really is well worth a visit. The main Nottingham to London railway runs through the area too and you have a fantastic view of a 1960s-built coal-fired power station, Radcliffe on Soar. It is also likely to be where the new High-Speed Rail Link comes thundering through. If that happens, then from one spot you will be able to view feats of engineering from the 18th, 19th, 20th and 21st century. As I say – well worth a visit!
55. Fear of water.

(second ball lost in 2 holes, good job he found so many on the 8th). Then I go. It is a thing of beauty sailing high over the lake and dropping onto the green within 10 feet. I miss the putt, but I don't care. The hole is a success in my eyes and, more importantly, Phil and I go 1 up in the match.

Jason, with a strong hint of surprise in his tone,[56] congratulates me on my success and then likens what I have just achieved to his role in life. I ask him to explain. "Well, as a pastor, part of my role is to spend time studying the Bible to understand what it meant *there*, in the time and the place it was written. Then with that understanding in place I can bring the teaching from *there* to *here*, our time and culture. Just as you were successful in getting the ball from there to here," as he points from the green, back over to the other side of the lake. "Then if I am successful in teaching, I have brought God's Word from *there* to *here*." I try to match his tone of surprise by saying, "Wow, that is profound," as if profundity from Jason was as rare[57] as good golf shots from me! It is clearly true though. God has preserved for us his Word, the Bible, that points us to Christ. However, we must be very careful in our handling of it. Too often we can carelessly quote or misquote it. We can take phrases out of context and manipulate them to meet our own passion of the moment. As the learned Dr Carl R. Trueman[58] (Dr Trueman to his friends) reminds us, if you string odd Bible verses together you can make it say whatever you want. For example, "Judas . . . went away

---

56. It is a little distressing to me how my playing partners always sound surprised when I play some decent golf! It does happen occasionally, as luck (or the random nature of my swing) would have it.
57. It isn't really.
58. This, I am sure, was in one of his many books, but for the moment I am unable to locate the reference.

and hanged himself,"[59] "Go and do likewise."[60] Do that sort of thing and we are failing to fly the lake and the ball just plops into the water with no further use to anyone. We do need people, like Jason, to be very careful in ensuring God's Word is accurately taken from *there* and appropriately taught and applied *here.*

The Bible is a truly remarkable book. It is the best attested ancient text. We have over 5,000 ancient Greek texts of the New Testament (not to mention the 86,000 very early Latin, Syrian and Egyptian translations). The earliest fragments we have date back to AD 150 within 70 or so years of the initial writing. Further, there is a consistency in all those texts, which destroys the myth that it has been changed or tampered with to any material degree. No other text comes close in its level of authentication. Caesar's Gallic War is the oft-quoted comparison where we have less than 10 texts dating from around 1,000 years after the events. Yet no one doubts Julius invaded Gaul, but we seem to want to doubt the stories about Jesus.[61]

We have got to ask the question "Why?" Why is God so concerned for us to have his Word and to be sure of its authenticity and authority. Dr J.I. Packer in his book *God Has Spoken* gives a superb answer:

"God's purpose is to make friends with us. It was to this end that he created us rational beings, bearing his image, able to think and hear and speak and love; he wanted there to be genuine personal affection and friendship, two sided, between himself and us – a relationship not like that between a man and his dog, but that of a parent to a

---

59. Matthew 27:5.
60. Luke 10:37.
61. Data taken from John Blanchard's book How to Enjoy Your Bible (Evangelical Press & Services Ltd, 2007).

child or husband and wife. Loving friendship between two persons has no ulterior motive; it is an end to itself."[62]

We walk off the 10th tee discussing the sublime, God's wonderful gift of the Bible. Things were about to revert to the ridiculous on the 11th.

A beautiful picture looking over the lake to the 10th green. The sight that strikes fear into all hydrophobic golfers!

62. Dr J.I. Packer, *God Has Spoken* (Hodder & Stoughton, 2016).

	Hole 10	Total
Par	4	
SI	7	
Phil (26)	8	53
SF	0	20
John (28)	6	54
SF	2	20
Jason (28)	7	53
SF	1	21
Brian (26)	7	52
SF	1	21

Match Play:
Phil and John
1 UP

In summary, the Fellowship of the "Fore" has made a Horlicks of this hole. Secretly I am not too displeased having won the hole, but shush, don't tell anyone.

Falling in Love with the Bible **by Mike Macintosh** (published by Victor). How to read the Bible as God's personal message to you.

Small But Significant

This book is primarily written for a Christian, golfing gentleman of my generation. If of that generation, you will remember the movie sensation of 1977. *STAR WARS*! We were the ones who queued for hours at our local cinema to watch the modern swash-buckling story of Luke Skywalker and friends taking on the might of the evil empire personified in the terrifying Darth Vader. *Star Wars* subsequently developed into a phenomenon that lives and breathes today. My favourite character in the first film is Biggs Darklighter. "Who?" you ask. Well, you can get a full biography of Darklighter from Wookieepedia the *Star Wars* Wiki. It seems he was a childhood friend of Skywalker and had a tiny part in the first film (*A New Hope*, Episode IV). However, that part was massively significant. He was a pilot in Red Squadron and in the final and desperate rebel attack on the Death Star he was shot down by Darth Vader. But here is the significance: he dragged Darth Vader away from Luke Skywalker's Star Fighter enabling Luke to complete the mission destroying the Death Star. Hooray, we were all on our seats cheering – back in the day! Biggs, you can see, had played a *small* but *significant* part in a galaxy far far away.

Having seeded that idea – "small but significant"– back to the round of golf. Hole 11 is the second easiest on the course (stroke index 17). It is a 280-yard par 4. The green is reachable in 2 shots even for golfers of our incompetence. It dog-legs gently left. There are several hazards: trees and cabbage down the left side, bunkers in position to catch a well-struck drive and, most notably, no space behind

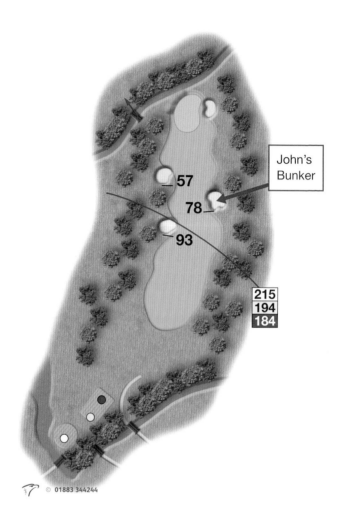

John's Bunker

57

78

93

215
194
184

© 01883 344244

the green. Anything too well struck will end up in a thick hawthorn hedge from which, to retrieve the ball, you'll be rewarded by a few thorns up the bum. The hedge is not shown on the map – but I assure you it is there.

Overall, the Fellowship of the "Fore" plays it well. After the first shot, only I am in trouble finding a fairway bunker. The other three all get green side in 2. My escape from the bunker costs and I end up with a 6. Brian and Jason take the hole, both managing to score 5 whereas Phil misses a 3-foot putt to end up, like me, with a 6. Considering all that has gone before on this round, this hole is relatively non-eventful.

However, there was a moment that stimulated my idea for this chapter. My ball was stuck in the bunker, a horrible position under the lip. Phil is much better at bunker escapes than I am. I would have loved to hand this task over to him. He gave me useful and encouraging advice (not): "just hit it and don't mess up". While in the bunker, to add to the tension I had to wait as a groundsman passed by riding his mowing machine. Then a member of the party behind decided to use our fairway; consequently, I had to wait some more. Now the moment had arrived, and it was down to me. No-one else was going to hit that shot. "Hit hard behind the ball taking some sand," I told myself. From the resultant sandstorm, my ball emerged safely out of the bunker and it made some progress down the fairway. Phil encouragingly observed, "Could have been better." I took that as high praise as I wiped sand out of my eyes and spat a little out of my mouth. "By the way," added Phil with a sardonic smile, "you should keep your mouth shut when hitting a bunker shot!" Helpful chap. I responded by politely reminding him of his marshmallow outfit as we moved on.

My thought, well, like Biggs Darklighter, I had a part to play. Consider all the activities around the golf course that morning. Groundsmen, receptionists, people working in the restaurant, those lovely administrators and, of course, all the players. In the totality of the picture, I am involved but only have a small part to play, but no-one else can play my part. If anybody did or if I wasn't there it would be different. Only Biggs had to opportunity to divert Darth

Vader. Only I can play my shots, including that horrible one out of the bunker.

Human life and Christian service is like that. We are all a small part of the enterprise. We all want to think that life is all about us and we are the hero of the movie. In reality, we are not. We are all Biggs Darklighters with small but significant parts to play.

Consider the big picture of the gospel. A loving creator God reaching out to a lost world. A magnificent plan of delivery centred on the person and work of Jesus. History is His Story. Think of the total span of human existence – over thousands of years – and ponder the geographical reach and scope of present gospel activity. Now into that picture fit yourself. One life, in one location for a limited period. I am sure you will agree – "small".

Yet the Bible tells us of a God who loves in detail. He cares about you, your life, your relationships, and your activity. In fact, he has prepared *in advance* works and tasks for you to do. It seems there are shots in the "gospel round" of golf only you can play.[63] It seems we all have a small but significant part to play in His Story.

This realisation gives us balance in life, service and our community. That balance of humility yet significance. We are all individually special and loved (like a child,[64] we are told) and have significance. Yet we are all individually playing a small part in the totality of God's plan. It is *not* ultimately all about us. As we consider that, then humility dawns in the same way as it does when that dreadful shot flies the green and gets stuck in the hawthorn hedge! Only I could have done that!

---

63. See Ephesians 2:10.
64. Biblically speaking we see our relationship with God in many ways. I always like to think that as we grow in faith our relationship becomes that of a mature child with our father. Still special and cared for but with capability, responsibility and accountability.

	Hole 11	Total
Par	4	
SI	17	
Phil (26)	6	59
SF	1	21
John (28)	6	60
SF	1	21
Jason (28)	5	58
SF	2	23
Brian (26)	5	57
SF	2	23

Match Play:

back to
ALL SQUARE

Hole 12

When it All Goes Wrong

From hole 11 it is a short walk through a gap in the hawthorn hedge to the 12th tee. There really is not a lot to hole 12. The course from hole 13 onwards becomes much more challenging. I refer to hole 12 as the "final sensible hole". It is a 192-yard par 3. Essentially a straight hit will get you on the fairway with a good opportunity to score a 3 or 4. Phil uses this as the opportune moment for a motivational team pep-talk. "Now is the time to extract the digit[65] and turn the screw[66] and not to be swinging the lead.[67]" The reason for this chain of idioms? Well, if you are following the match play situation you will recognise that with Phil and me losing hole 11 the match is all square again. This is making Phil nervous and, when nervous, he reverts to speaking in idioms. So, with his own articulate pep-talk ringing in his ears, Phil strikes his drive down the fairway, as do Brian and Jason. Not great shots but all ok.

Up to this point I have played reasonably well (a pleasant surprise for Phil). My score is not a personal all time low, but it is, statistically, in the lower quadrant of my recent performances. So, with some degree of confidence, I hit

---

65. Idioms of the English language. "Extract the digit" is our version of "pull your finger out". Visitors to the HMS *Victory* in Portsmouth are told that "the expression 'pull your finger out' came about as an instruction to 'powder monkeys' (the young lads who loaded cannons on British Navy warships) to remove their finger from the cannon's fuse to allow the cannon to be fired".
66. "Turn the screw" is a rather distasteful reference to the use of thumbscrews.
67. "Swinging the lead" another idiom from the British Navy. It seems before the days of sonar the depth of water was determined by dropping a lead weight from the front of the ship. The weight was attached to a calibrated rope (by means of knots or marking). The constant dropping and lifting of the weight was hard work. It seems occasionally this duty was neglected and the lead was allowed to swing and the sailors called out imaginary depths. Do this for too long and the ship could be heading for a bunker full of rocks!

the tee-shot. It is an unmitigated disaster. I catch the ball with the toe-end of my 5-iron and it travels 10 feet to the right coming to rest in a patch of horribly thick and damp grass. I look to Jason and Brian for mercy but as the match play situation is so close no grace is on offer (see hole 5). *This underlines the fickle nature of human grace. It is not eternal like the divine version.* My second shot is doomed from the start. In fact, I do quite well to simply move the ball out of the grass. In playing the shot I scythe a huge amount of grass, some of which ends up on my head and some of which makes more progress down the fairway than my ball. Looking scarecrow-like I am now feeling frustrated, a little embarrassed and very glad I am playing with good friends. Who, at that moment, were sharing the unspoken dilemma: is now a good time for a witty comment? I am sure I overheard the name "Worzel Gummidge" uttered, but to give Jason his due it was whispered in a sympathetic tone.

Having made very little progress with the first two shots I need to make the third special. I "give it the beans"[68] with my hybrid. The ball flies high but then it turns right (a nasty slice). "Fore right" is the hearty cry. The ball clears the trees right of the green and lands in the small ditch. This is now a complete disaster hole – it is all going wrong! A drop followed by a recovery shot out onto the fairway results in my 6th shot getting to the edge of the green. I pick up (a golfing term for "giving up"). The score we write on the card is "6" which is sufficient for zero Stableford points (in our golfing terms: "a blob"). We all recognise that this is

---

68. "Give it the beans" originates from the birth place of democracy. It seems that in ancient Greece voting was by means of putting beans into jars. To "give it the beans" was to be committed to that idea or course of action. In golfing terms, it means to put everything into the shot. Usually with unwanted consequences.

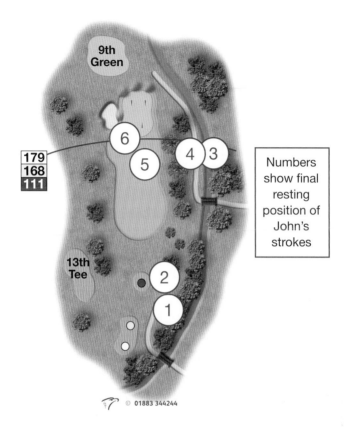

not accurate use of data but one ridiculously bad hole (as this one is) can do so much damage to fragile egos when reviewing the score in the clubhouse. We offer each other that degree of mercy.

Phil's "4" matches that of Jason's and Brian's, resultantly the match play situation remains all square. For me, though, the round has gone wrong. In our golf round of faith, what do we make of situations that seem to go all wrong? Difficulties and challenges come our way. Some of our own making and some completely out of our control.

Difficulties, challenges, suffering and sadness, it seems, are part of our human lot. However, we have to ask two questions: (1) why? and (2) where is God when things go wrong?

This is a huge subject and not one that I am capable of fully understanding or adequately debating. I did consider simply leaving this subject out and finding some other, more palatable and humorous, topic for hole 12. That, though, would be a big miss as things do go wrong on the golf course of life and the Christian faith has much comfort and support to give in such situations.

To try and answer the first question: "Why?" Well, we can give a couple of general answers. Firstly, we live in a fallen world with the resultant distortion of the created order. A world in which we have beauty and ugliness, calm and storm, a seeming randomness to events which favours some and victimises others. Secondly, through the events of this mad, bad, sin-sick, fallen world, we see God working his perfect purposes out. The Apostle Paul (one who suffered much) concluded: *"I consider that our present sufferings are not worth comparing with the glory that will be revealed in us."*[69] Somehow, Paul is proposing that in God's economy, all the weight of human suffering will be as nothing compared to the value and worth of what God has in plan.

While to people of faith these are good answers, they are only ever generalisations. They say nothing of particular suffering and difficulties. General answers are never wholly satisfactory. We could give gravity as a reason for the Twin Towers falling on 11th September 2001. While true, it does not tell the whole story as to why those *particular* towers

69. Romans 8:18.

fell on that *particular* day.[70] We all would like specific answers to understand our own challenges and difficulties. Rarely, though, do we get them. Yes, we can see how good is worked from wretched situations. I can think of the untimely death of a young man I knew well and the immediate pain for all of us around him. In time, though, I can see how great good came of that situation. If we could sit on the arc of the universe and see the beginning from the end then, perhaps, we could see how God sees things and then a level of understanding would dawn.

In faith, though, we must accept the generalisations and trust that God is, mysteriously, working his purposes out even in and through our lives. Sometimes that is to our temporal benefit and sometimes not. Hebrews chapter 11 is known as the "Gallery of Faith". A list of biblical characters who lived their lives trusting God. Towards the end of the chapter (verses 32 to 40), we have a rapid-fire list of people and events. There is a stark dichotomy between verses 32 to 35a and 35a to 38. The first group (32 to 35a) all seemed to have received temporal blessing. They *conquered kingdoms, administered justice, weakness turned to strength, became powerful in battle, and routed foreign armies, rescued from the mouth of lions, received their dead raised to life.* The second group (35a to 38) seemed to have no temporal blessing but much suffering. They were *tortured, jeered, flogged, chained, imprisoned, stoned, sawn in two, executed by the sword. They went about in sheepskins, destitute, persecuted, and ill-treated.* Yet, and here is the key point, they were all commended for their faith and will receive the same eternal blessing.

---

70. Illustration taken from Carl R. Trueman's *The Rise and Triumph of the Modern Self* (Crossway, 2020).

Earthly success really is not the determinant of heavenly blessing. In honesty, I cannot give a fully rounded answer to the "why" question. Many great thinkers, philosophers and theologians have tried and ended up concluding much the same. As humans on this planet, we have a choice between the randomness of a pointless existence or faith in a greater one than ourselves who has a plan and gives purpose to our lives.

The second question: "Where is God when things go wrong?" This one is much easier to answer. He is here with us. God became man. A baby born in Bethlehem. As such he walked our road and he shared our pain. *"Tempted in every way, just as we are."*[71] The message of the gospel is that he suffered in our place. Not only sharing our pain but taking the greater part of it for us. God has not detached himself from a suffering world; no, completely the opposite. He has joined us in the difficulties and challenges so that his purposes may be fulfilled. In that particular and temporal sense that I referenced above, Jesus promised that he will walk alongside each one of us in easy and difficult times.[72] Many a person has testified to knowing more of God's presence and spiritual blessing in the difficult and trying times of their lives than when things are going well. My father was an illegitimate child raised by a single parent in the grinding poverty and judgemental society of 1930s Britain. His favourite Bible verse was God's promise to be a *"father to the fatherless"*.[73] He testified to knowing God's presence with him as he walked through many a difficult situation.

---

71. Hebrews 4:15.
72. In Matthew 28:20 Jesus promises to be with us *"always, to the very end of the age"*.
73. Psalm 68:5.

In golfing terms, God has come and joined us on our round and shares in our frustrations and difficulties. We can view him as the stronger partner supporting us on our way. Coaching, encouraging and sharing in the emotion of every shot, every difficulty and every triumph. He is our Shepherd, Brother, Friend, Prophet, Priest and King. Our Lord, our Life, our Way, our End.[74] May he accept the praise and service we bring.

---

74. Taken from the hymn "How Sweet the Name of Jesus Sounds" by John Newton.

	Hole 12	Total
Par	3	
SI	11	
Phil (26)	4	62
SF	2	24
John (28)	6	66
SF	0	21
Jason (28)	4	62
SF	2	25
Brian (26)	4	61
SF	2	25

Match Play:

ALL SQUARE

Suffering is part of life. Christianity has much to offer us at those most difficult times. Can I recommend: *Hope in the Face of Suffering* **by Jeremy Marshall** (10 Publishing). *A Journey Through Cancer* **by John Ellwood** (Malcolm Down Publishing).

Hole 13

Miracles Do Happen

My daughter bought me a birthday card. On the front it stated: "Happy Birthday to a golf-playing dad. When it goes right it is a slice, when it goes left it is a hook." Then inside the card it read: "When it goes straight it is a ******* miracle." I have already mentioned that miracles do happen, well on this round we had a couple. All of us managing a score of 4 on hole 3 was the first and the standard of our play on this hole was the second.

The 13th is stroke index 1,[75] a 427-yard par 4. If you were a professional and you played this hole in regulation, then shot 1 is an easy a 200-yard plus drive (target golf for a professional) to get you alongside a small thin lake. The vast array of huge trees stops anyone from attempting to cut the corner. Shot 2 is an iron to cover the remaining 200 yards to hit the green. Shot 3 is a medium-size putt to within a couple of feet of the hole. Shot 4 is a tap-in for a par. Well, that is the theory at least.

We are not professionals and the theory does not, usually, work out in practice. We generally take two or three shots to get over the lake and a further three or four to get in the hole. Many a ball has hit the middle of the lake (too far from the bank even for ball saviour Phil to come to the rescue), and there has been many a search for balls in the rough, followed by many a frustrated hack just trying to recover some sort of position on the fairway. This hole usually saps all hope, making you resign yourself to a

---

75. That means it is believed by the course designers to be the most difficult hole on the course.

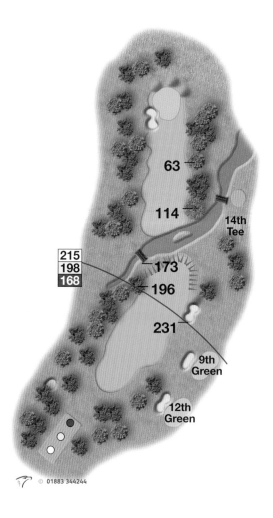

© 01883 344244

blob (zero Stableford points) while still some distance from the hole.

This day was different; this day was not the same.[76] Both Phil and I hit cracking drives into prime position for getting over the lake. I strike a beautiful 7-iron and make the green. Phil follows suit. That is miracle enough and

---

76. To quote another progressive rock song.

draws a quivering of the marshmallow suit in celebration. I take two, so the above-mentioned professional regulation plan comes true. Phil, however, rolls the putt home. Major marshmallow action! Miracle upon miracle we have a birdie on stroke index 1 and **5 Stableford points**. Jason and Brian manage a 5 and a 6. On any normal day very respectable, but today – simply not good enough. Phil, feeling a little faint, considers retiring to the clubhouse at that moment where he can make his achievements sound even more incredible. *For many months after he continued to remind everyone of this achievement – not surprising – so would I.*

It is the hope of occasionally playing holes in regulation that keeps us going and trying. It is said that in every round there is at least one shot that gives you the hope that next time something special will happen. Often that hope is dashed on the rocks of poor shots, rubbish decisions and rotten technique. In a golfing sense I am putting my vain hope in me and my limited abilities. Delivery is rare, so rare, that I describe it as a miracle when I make a par.

Christian hope is entirely different. It is presented in sharp contrast to the variability of the hope offered by this world. The world promises but rarely delivers. Yet, Christ provides a sure and certain hope and will always deliver. This hope is not founded in what we may be able to achieve, on a good day. No, this hope is founded on what he has *already* achieved.

Phillips Brooks, the writer of "O Little Town of Bethlehem", was not far from the mark when he commented that "all the armies that ever marched, all the navies that ever sailed, all the parliaments that ever sat, all the kings that ever reigned, put together have not affected the life of man on earth as has this one solitary life".[77]

---

77. Robert J. Morgan, *Nelson's Complete Book of Stories, Illustrations and Quotes* (Trust Media Distribution, 2000).

H.G. Wells, the novelist, stated, "I am a historian, I am not a believer. But this penniless preacher from Galilee is irresistibly the centre of humanity."[78]

The Bible is very clear that this man Jesus is no less than the incarnate God. "The hopes and fears of all the years"[79] rest on him. He has completed his task. In a golfing sense he has perfectly completed his round. Further, by the grace of God and the gift of faith his score is attributed to us. That is why Christian hope is in no way like the emotion I have when hitting a shot. Placing my hope in the random nature of an insecure swing. No, in Christ I am placing my hope in the one true God. I am placing my hope in something that has been achieved and the one who has achieved it and the one who continues to work his purposes out. This hope is sure, unshakeable, eternal and it is a glorious miracle!

---

78. Thomas A. Harris, *I'm OK – You're OK* (New York: Quill, 2004).
79. Taken from "O Little Town of Bethlehem" by Phillips Brooks (1835–1893).

	Hole 13	Total
Par	4	
SI	1	
Phil (26)	3	66
SF	5	28
John (28)	4	70
SF	4	25
Jason (28)	5	67
SF	3	28
Brian (26)	6	67
SF	2	27

Match Play:

Phil and John
1 UP

Truly magnificent scoring by the Fellowship of the "Fore" on this hole. At this point Phil takes a lead on all forms of scoring. We all doubted it would continue.

***Fresh Footprints* by John Houghton** (Malcolm Down Publishing). What is the evidence for a God that can work miracles? Well, have a read.

Hole 14

I Talk to the Wind

"Give me a man with big hands, big feet and no brains . . . I will make a golfer out of him."[80]

There are many quips about the futility of the game and the stupidity of the people that play it. Golf, it famously seems, "spoils a good walk". On those bad rounds, especially when it is cold and wet, I do vaguely question why I do it. There is a level of compulsion. Somehow the next shot, next hole, next round will be better. There is also the sheer joy of it, too. Being with good mates and away from the pressures and events of the real world. For 3 to 4 hours all that matters is tee to hole (18 times) and banter with those good mates. Which brings me to hole 14.

We are now well into the second half of the round. Fully engaged, still far enough from the end of the round to be worrying about reality and the match is on a highly enjoyable knife edge. Phil's miracle birdie on the 13th has restored our 1-hole lead. The tension is at a palpable pitch. Fortunately hole 14 runs the other side of the toilet (as described during hole 8) so there is the potential of relief for our frayed nerves and filling bladders.

I like hole 14, a gentle dog-leg right, par 4, 338 yards. To its advantage it is stroke index 4 which entitles me to 2 strokes. To complete it in 6 is a par at my level of incompetence. However, to its disadvantage is that we are on the more exposed part of the course and the wind whistles off the River Trent and does some cruel things to

---

80. Quote attributed to Walter Hagen. Taken from *A Little Bit of Golfing Wit* by Tom Hay (Summersdale, 2018).

the flight of the ball. Hence the need for all good golfers to be "wind-talkers". Many golfers are "ball-talkers" too. It is a skill only mastered by the few! Here on hole 14, removed from reality, wind and ball-talking become significant. As you will see.

On the tee the wind is coming at us from the left. Phil (with the honour, after his birdie on the 13th) strikes first. He just reminds us that he has the honour because of his miracle birdie and it is clear he is still a little faint from the experience. The marshmallow ensemble is all of a dither! Surprisingly, the drive is good but it gets pushed to the right by the wind. It is heading to the toilet. "Very convenient,"[81] observes Brian.

I go next. It is a good contact. The ball's flight is high and left, so the wind-talking begins:

"Blow, wind, blow."

"Push the ball right."

Amazingly it complies and the ball pulls right, straight into the fairway bunker around 200 yards away. Jason, the man who needs no wind to make his ball fly left to right, follows a similar route but annoyingly avoids the bunker. I note he did not instruct the wind at all. A lesson I should have noted. Finally, Brian hits a tracer bullet of a drive no more than a foot off the ground down the centre, thereby avoiding any wind interference. Brian, though, is heard ordering the ball to "keep going" to get beyond the tree line so he has a chance of hitting his second shot into the green. The ball does not obey and pulls up short just a few yards ahead of the bunker my wind-assisted ball has found.

---

81. There are various course legends around golfers being struck by errant golf balls while enjoying the relief of the toilet. I can testify to finding a golf ball in the toilet once. I left it there – not wanting to rescue that one!

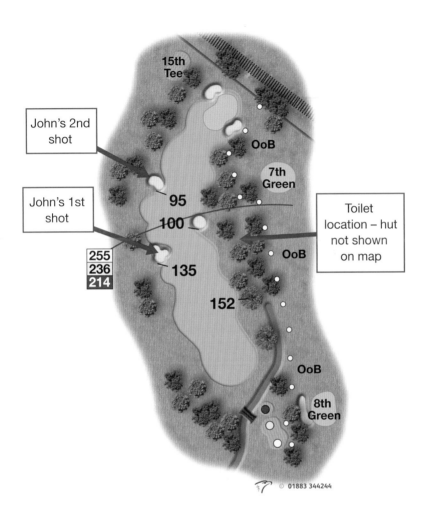

15th
Tee

John's 2nd
shot

OoB

7th
Green

John's 1st
shot

95

100

Toilet
location – hut
not shown
on map

255
236
214

135

OoB

152

OoB

8th
Green

© 01883 344244

I am in another bunker! Unbelievable! "Please feel free to use all bunker facilities on the course," utters Phil as he leaves me in the sand and heads over to the other facility. My bunker escape is good. The ball, though, is flying directly towards the next bunker. Not to worry, I think, the wind will blow. "Blow, wind, blow!" I shout. This time no movement at all, and, plop! The ball drops into the centre of the next deep bunker. It has dropped from a significant height and now looks a little like a fried egg as the ball is snuggly buried in the sand. "Why, wind, why?" I ask.

We all, in procession, then make progress to the green. I arrive with my fourth shot after taking the punishment of the fried-egg shot. The other three are there in 3. Then the ball-talking really begins. Phil putts, it looks like it is going to be short. "Go, ball, go." It does. "Stop, ball, stop." It does not. Fortunately, he manages to hole the return and halves the hole in 5. My fifth shot is a long putt but certainly not without hope. In surveying the green, I conclude there is a left-to-right movement. I send the ball on its way, perfect weight, I think. "Turn right, ball, right, RIGHT!" The dumb ball decides to keep straight and then disobeys completely and wobbles left as it comes to a halt. I give it a severe talking to before holing out for a 6.

My mind wanders back to King Crimson who wrote a song that referenced "talking to the wind" but concluded that the wind cannot hear. They must have been playing golf while writing that song.

We seem to spend a lot of time talking to things that cannot hear. Psalm 135 notes that idols have ears but cannot hear.[82] It highlights the futility of speaking to an idol. As mad as a golfer talking to the wind or shouting at a ball. Is praying to an invisible God equally absurd? I wonder about the quote I use at the start of this chapter. Are Christians people with big hands, feet and hearts (keen to serve and do good) but no real sense? Further, is praying as senseless as shouting at a rolling ball or beseeching the wind to come to one's aid?

To answer let us consider Jesus, who is reported by the gospel writers to have prayed regularly. If it is madness

---

82. Psalm 135:17.

to pray then you must consider Jesus to be mad. Mad, bad or God?[83] If we have concluded Jesus is God then we have to believe in and practise prayer. Jesus taught us a lot about prayer. He taught his disciples how to pray (regularly, naturally, believingly[84]) and He encourages us to pray and keep on praying.[85] We believe in a God who is keen to listen to our prayers.[86] A living God who, unlike the wind, can hear and will listen. We too often think about prayer as if it is a shopping list of requests. I believe we should understand it to be much more an exercise in faith and a series of relationship-building conversations with our heavenly Father. My children are all grown up now and our conversations are an extension and strengthening of our relationship. Gone are the requests for ice-cream or the latest computer game (they are fully capable of providing those for themselves). So it can be with God. In prayer we can discuss everything with him. Yes, we can bring our needs to him and he is the one who will give us good things,[87] he is the one we can trust. However, even if we make no requests and receive no answers, prayer remains that ongoing conversation with God. A remarkable gift earnt for us by Jesus. We are encouraged to boldly approach God. An unbelievable privilege.[88]

We are mad to talk to the blowing wind and the rolling ball, but there is no madness in speaking with the Living God. We should do it more. Charles Spurgeon remarked, "I cannot remember praying for longer than 20 minutes but neither can I remember 20 minutes without prayer."

83. Or "lunatic, liar or Lord" as C.S. Lewis famously expressed the question.
84. Matthew 6:5-15.
85. Luke 18:1-8.
86. Matthew 7:7-12.
87. James 1:17.
88. Hebrews 10:19.

We can be 21st-century Christian men who speak not to the wind but to the God in heaven who loves to hear us pray. Although, I wouldn't mind if the wind would listen, at least once.

	Hole 14	Total
Par	4	
SI	5	
Phil (26)	5	70
SF	3	32
John (28)	6	76
SF	2	27
Jason (28)	5	72
SF	3	31
Brian (26)	5	72
SF	3	30

Match Play:
Phil and John remain 1 UP

Prayer is the cornerstone of our ongoing relationship with God. Well worth reading some more on the subject. Can I recommend *Teach Us to Pray by Rob White* (Malcolm Down Publishing).

The Big Shot

Holes 15, 16 and 17, running parallel to the River Trent, are at the extreme point of the course with the 15th tee being furthest away from the clubhouse. If you avoid concentrating on the middle-aged men waving their clubs about, it really is a picture-postcard spot. There is a well-used footpath and cycle way between the golf course and the river. Behind the 15th tee is a multi-arched railway bridge through which grazing cows can be seen on a large area of pasture. This leads to a small village and a pretty church boasting an English-style steeple. All in all, on one of those all-too-rare bright days it is good to be alive on the 15th tee. On the all-too-often wet and windy days it is the most exposed spot and you need to get off the tee box as quickly as possible to preserve your life. The vagaries of English weather.[89]

With the footpath and cycle way along the right, those passing walkers and cyclists provide lots of opportunities for us to joke about taking them out with a sliced drive or discussing what the rules would require if we managed to bounce a ball off a passing cyclist's helmet back onto the fairway.[90]

On this day the walkers were numerous and gathered to watch us hit our drives. I scuffed one down the middle, that received a moderate round of applause. Phil followed

---

89. During my career I travelled to Thailand on numerous occasions. My Thai colleagues constantly ask me about the English weather and the constant rain. The joke being that Thailand is so much better served with weather than England. I respond by saying, "England has the best weather in the world, but we only have a few days of it."
90. See section 11 Rules of Golf, effective January 2019, R&A and USGA.

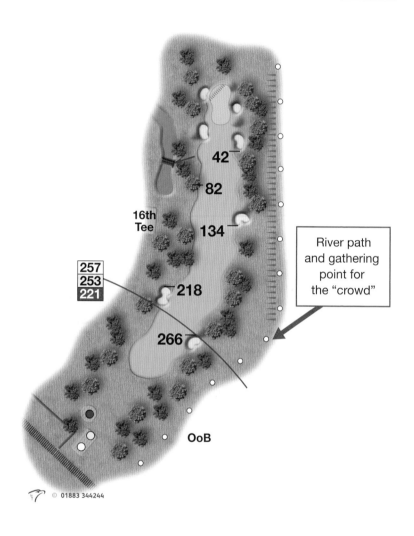

16th Tee

42

82

134

257
253
221

218

266

River path and gathering point for the "crowd"

OoB

© 01883 344244

receiving a similar level of appreciation. Brian hits one directly at the crowd but falling short of his target into the rough and trees on the right. This brought an "ooh" and "aah" from the gathering. The excitement was reaching fever pitch (not) as Jason took the stage and unleashed a classic. The contact was perfect, a tuneful "ping" off the club and the ball sails majestically onwards. It flies alongside a passing squadron of geese (regular visitors to the course) for a beautiful few microseconds. Then it falls impacting the fairway, smack in the middle, a good 250-300 yards away. The crowd are impressed and deliver a rousing ovation. A muted "you're the man" was heard. Jason takes a bow and we move on down the fairway and the crowd go on their way clearly believing Jason is the professional lowering himself to play with lesser golf mortals.

Hole 15 is a 484-yard par 5, the fairway bends gently left. Like all fairways at Trent Lock it is tight with hazards on both sides. Jason's next shot is long but straight into the water; his recovery is not good, chipping into a bunker. The three of us considered calling the crowd back so they could see Jason's true golf identity. My second and third are both surprisingly straight. My fourth takes me to the green and I only take two more. Brian and Phil both play the rest of the hole well. As his ball drops (for a par that wins the hole) Brian enunciates our thoughts, "Shame the crowd did not see that!" "Jason the Crowd Pleaser" ends up with a 7. My conclusion to the escapade is – what the crowd did not see was far more important, in the final analysis, than what they did see.

Isn't that so true of our Christian walk? What matters most is what happens away from the gaze of the crowd. God's priority is the content of our character and the desires of our hearts. Really only known to God and us. We are saved by grace through faith in Christ and we have those good works prepared in advance for us to do.[91] Yet the life we have is full of opportunities to live a sham. To provide the outside world with a good show while inside the rot is setting in. In golf terms: "drive for show but putt

91. Ephesians 2:8-10. See also hole 11.

for dough". Jesus was particularly critical of the Pharisees and teachers of the law. Surprisingly (!?) he does not use a golfing analogy, preferring to reference cups that are clean on the outside but all dirty, full of greed and self-indulgence, on the inside.[92]

We need to be asking for constant help in this respect that God's will is worked out in our lives and we continue to follow the example of "The Man"[93] by living authentic lives where what is seen on the outside is a true reflection of what is going on inside.

To conclude, in life the big shots are not, usually, those that are constantly getting our attention but very much those who do good for others and are often only fully appreciated after their work is fully done. Not too dissimilar from Christ?

A view across the 15th green towards the 16th fairway. Phil's most hated spot on the course! "It always goes wrong here," he says.

92. Matthew 23:25-26.
93. Philippians 2:1-5.

	Hole 15	Total
Par	5	
SI	15	
Phil (26)	6	77
SF	2	34
John (28)	6	82
SF	2	29
Jason (28)	7	79
SF	1	32
Brian (26)	5	77
SF	3	33

Match Play:
ALL SQUARE
(again)

After the indifferent drive Brian played an excellent hole. This brings the match back to all square, so the gentle competition I noted on the first hole is beginning to become tense. Not sure I can describe it as "gentle" anymore.

Complaints to the Hon-Sec

John S, one of our good mates playing in the threesome ahead of us, often jokes about the need for a "strongly worded letter to the Hon-Sec". The Honorary Secretary is the fictional guiding counsel for the management of the course. We have a long list of reasonable things to complain about:

- Too many leaves on the course

- Not enough sand in the bunkers

- Too much sand in the bunkers

- The wrong type of sand in the bunkers[94]

- Overhanging branches on trees

- Goose poo on the paths

- Fairways cut too short

- Fairways not cut short enough

- Curmudgeonly swans who won't move to allow access to your ball *(they can get quite violent, so some danger there which is not to be underestimated)*

- Cabbage too thick

---

94. The USGA recommend as a general guideline, that sand used in bunkers should be composed of particles with a large majority in the range of 0.25-1.00mm. Silt and clay (particles below 0.05mm) should be kept to a minimum, since they are associated with surface crusting. I really cannot cope with surface crusting!

- Too many thorns in the hedges (which end up stuck in us)

- Sprinklers coming on at the wrong time

- Too much wind (external and internal?!)

- Groundsmen that drive across the fairway we are playing on, not once, but many times! They claim to be mowing. I am sure the grass will not grow to preposterous lengths by the time we'd finish our round.

- Other members not suitably attired (not to mention Phil's marshmallow outfit – see hole 1, and various other references, if you have unbelievably forgotten)

But the chief complaint I have is the positioning of holes. I cannot tell you the number of times when I have hit a shot so beautifully onto the green that would have resulted in momentous scoring if only the hole was in the correct place. As you may recall from hole 4, I mentioned the propensity of the green keepers for putting holes on the side of slopes. If you keep reading you will realise why I mention this again in this long and meandering introduction to hole 16.

Hole 16, although officially stroke index 9, is the most difficult hole on the course (in the opinion of the Fellowship of the "Fore"); a 487-yard par 5. The difficulty comes not from the length but the terrain. It is necessary to hit the tee shot straight and high to travel the 170 yards to a small peninsula with water on three sides (that is the definition of a peninsula – I just add the definition in case you had forgotten or never knew). Of course, as a peninsula the ground runs out. So, if you hit too good a drive you can enter the water at the far side. Once on the peninsula you need to get off it again, followed by a danger ridden traversal of a narrow fairway with bunkers and a river on the right and trees and cabbage on the left. At the end of the fairway more water to pitch over before arriving on a green with slopes and a hole which is always . . . IN THE WRONG POSITION!

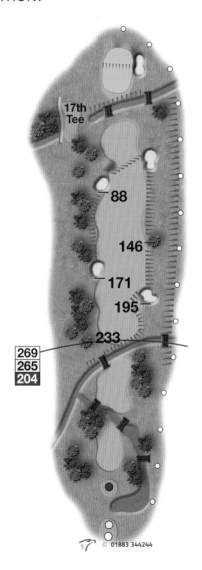

17th
Tee

88

146

171

195

233

269
265
204

01883 344244

Faced with this formidable challenge we are all somewhat nervous each time we stand on the 16th tee. Usually, we fail to score any Stableford points carding an 8 or a 9 depending on our handicaps. It sometimes feels like it is a waste of time trying after finding the water with shot 1, taking a drop (shot 2) and finding the second set of water with shot 3 which then requires a further drop. Four shots down and still not off the peninsula. Well, for this round it goes remarkably well for me (lucky really). The tee shot hooks and lands short of the water in horrible cabbage. The hack out narrowly avoids the water at the extreme edge of the peninsula. The ball now though is positioned perfectly for my 4-iron to smack it (a fantastic shot) way down the centre of the fairway. My fourth shot is a pitch to within 5 feet of the hole. "Blimey," I think, "I can par hole 16" (5 for 3 for **4** Stableford points!). My excitement is building. The hole is, of course, positioned half-way down a gentle slope. After spending a few moments reading the green (I've watched the professionals do it!), I conclude there is a small right-to-left swing on the putt.[95] I gently send it on its way, it turns just as expected, gliding towards the hole, but it does not drop. It catches the front of the hole then proceeds to balance on the edge for a 240-degree dance around the hole, coming to rest hanging over the hole on the left side. Unbelievable! I chunter on about a further letter to the Hon-Sec for the rotten hole position. This could never have happened if the hole was not on the side of a slope. The ball looks up at me with a smug Callaway smile.[96] That ball has been thrown into the bottom of my bag where it still resides as a fair and just punishment for its part in this heinous crime.

95. "Put" means to place an object where you want it. "Putt" is the inability to achieve this!
96. The Callaway logo does look a little like a smile; it laughs at my attempts to hit it.

Even though I win the hole my playing colleagues share my pain. They, in one accord, agree that a further letter of complaint is most certainly justified. The conversation then turns to the full list of complaints that we have, as listed above (there are many more, I am just working hard on being concise to avoid boring you too much). Then we notice the sun shining, admire the autumnal trees in all their glorious colours, feel the gentle breeze and take in the fact that we are playing a round of golf while looking forward to the bacon cob in the clubhouse afterwards. Contentment soon returns.

There is an old hymn which we never sing now (reading the arcane language I can understand why) but it reminds us of the minor and transitory nature of our complaints versus the reality of our physical and spiritual state.

When upon life's billows you are tempest-tossed,
When you are discouraged, thinking all is lost,
Count your many blessings, name them one by one,
And it will surprise you what the Lord has done.[97]

The psalmists often complained (check out psalms 2, 82 and 142 for example) but as you read you will note that their complaining is often turned to appreciation and praise of God. When we consider what Christ has won for us and how vast and overwhelming God's love is, I mean, really, what have we got to complain about? See Philippians 4:10-12.

Having said that and trying to encourage you to look to God and count your blessings – I am still pondering on God's purpose for preventing my putt from dropping on the 16th. Perhaps I need to let it go? And learn to be content?

---

97. "Count Your Blessings" by Johnson Oatman (1856–1922).

	Hole 16	Total
Par	5	
SI	9	
Phil (26)	8	85
SF	0	33
John (28)	6	88
SF	3	32
Jason (28)	7	86
SF	2	34
Brian (26)	7	84
SF	1	34

Match Play:
Phil and John return to 1 UP

I am delighted to have made another contribution by winning this hole. Phil is very surprised but equally delighted. Just two holes to go!

Hole 17

Mr S or Mr C?

Still feeling a little sore about the missed putt on the 16th and the outrageous injustice of the hole placement, I wander onto the tee for hole 17. Hole 17 is a 320-yard par 4 with a right-angled dog-leg left. 200 yards from the tee is a small lake with a narrow crossing point (not really a bridge, it is essentially part of the fairway). Then another 50 yards on is the turn to the small green. Standing on the tee there is a choice to be made. You can take an iron and lay-up, knowing you will need a second to get over the lake, or you can take the "big-dog" from the bag and try to smash the ball over the lake.

I remember on at least one occasion I have succeeded (I guess it could have been a dream, but it was very vivid). I am also acutely aware that I usually fail. There are, at this critical point of decision, two voices in my head. Mr Sensible says: "Lay-up, you know it is the right thing to do. Just think how you will feel when you fail – again!" Mr Courageous (otherwise known as Mr Stupid) says: "Go for it. Think of the glory!" The battle with the temptation is furious. I keep changing the club I half-pull out of the bag. My playing chums know my dilemma and fuel the fire.

Jason: "You've been driving well today, John. Might be worth a go."

Brian: "I've seen you do it before and you do need a good score on this hole."

The temptation is real, I visualise the ball flying high and mighty. I see it landing the other side of the lake and lapping up the fairway as it closes in on the green. I then listen to Mr Sensible and remember how I always feel when the ball flies high and not so mighty and plops, limply, into the centre of the lake.

It is while I am enduring this mental torment that we behold a remarkable site. A driverless electric golf trolley fully loaded is coming our way (it seems we are witnessing a scene from the future). It steers itself over the bridge, avoiding the lake and crashes into the hedge on the right side of the fairway. Trolley wheels still frantically spinning. Then a second remarkable site. Three older men walking at pace towards the lake all searching for the tell-tale signs of a sunk trolley, bag and clubs. It seems the threesome ahead of us were just finishing up on the green when John W could not find his bag to replace his putter. Panic and frantic scanning of the immediate vicinity ensued, without success. All they could conclude was that the fully loaded trolley must have met a watery end.

We (the Fellowship of the "Fore") did discuss how long we should leave them in panic stations, feverishly scanning the lake for ripples or signs of sunken clubs, before pointing out the energetic trolley in the hedge (with wheels still spinning). I suggested we tee-off deliberately trying to hit the water, scoring additional points if we successfully splashed them. Phil concluded that our concern for their cardiac well-being should shorten our fun and firing balls into the water was "beyond the pale" (idiom chosen to maintain the watery theme).[98] We went to rescue the

---

98. Upon researching this idiom it seems it has nothing to do with a pail of water. It originates from medieval Ireland where the eastern side was under British rule. The western side was under Irish rule and known as the "Pale". Hence "beyond the Pale" became an idiom indicating behaviour outside the bounds of acceptability.

trolley and a relieved John W started to breathe again. "You really could not write this stuff," he said . . . and that gave me an idea.

All this drama delayed my decision and ultimately, I couldn't resist and took the driver. I smack it hard but pull it left. I am not in the lake, but neither am I in front of the green. I end up left of the fairway and at the base of a thick bush (an area of the course I had never visited before). I need to take two more shots to get in position for the green. Feeling, as always, guilty for failing to stand strong against the temptation. Mr Sensible is giving me a serious talking to and Mr Stupid has retired from the scene. Of course, I am sure you never doubted it, Jason, Phil and Brian all play sensibly and do not yield to the temptation and end up scoring better than I do.

We all have choices to make every day. We can choose to be selfish or selfless, proud or humble, judgemental or forgiving, taking or giving. We hear those conflicting conversations in our mind. Life is a complex web of cause and consequence and each of us with the constant support of prayer and the help of the Holy Spirit must work our way through. There are many trials and temptations and there is trouble everywhere.[99] We have periods stuck in the rough and we must endure trolley crashes and times of worry and loss (see hole 12).

We are told that we will not be tempted beyond our capabilities to resist and that when tempted there will always be an alternative course we can take. We do have a choice![100]

---

99. To quote the famous hymn "What a Friend We Have in Jesus" by Joseph Scriven (1819–1886).
100. 1 Corinthians 10:13.

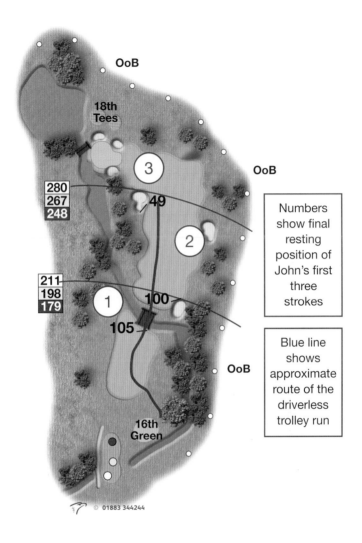

OoB

18th
Tees

3

OoB

280
267
248

49

2

Numbers
show final
resting
position of
John's first
three
strokes

211
198
179

1

100

105

Blue line
shows
approximate
route of the
driverless
trolley run

OoB

16th
Green

© 01883 344244

We are also told that we have a Great High Priest who
has been tempted in every way like us, yet is without sin.
He chose to be selfless; he chose to be humble, he chose
to forgive, and he chose to give; he gave himself fully and
completely. Now that passage in Hebrews 4 tells us that he

can sympathise with us in our weakness and longs to help us in our times of need.[101]

Drawing this loose analogy between a round of golf and living out the Christian life, then, we have with us a constant coach[102] who knows what we are going through and is willing to guide and lead by example. Metaphorically speaking I am sure that if I listened to him on the 17th tee, I would not be hacking out of the deep rough with my second shot. I guess for many of us that scenario has played out many times in our lives. Let's strive, more and more, to follow his guidance and example to avoid those temptations, sand-traps and huge stretches of rough that the world, the flesh and the devil will put in our way.

Finally, though, I must add. We will all fail at some point and when we do, we have a faithful friend who will be there to pick us up again.

---

101. Hebrews 4:14-16.
102. Please note I do not intend to in anyway here reduce the majesty and wonder of Jesus; with this image my hope is to magnify it. He is primarily our Lord. However, the wonder of our relationship with him is that he is many other things too. To quote, again, John Newton, he is "my Shepherd, Brother, Friend. My Prophet, Priest and King. My Lord, my Life, my Way, my End". His guidance and example are there for all of us, should we choose to accept it.

	Hole 17	Total
Par	4	
SI	3	
Phil (26)	6	91
SF	2	35
John (28)	7	95
SF	1	33
Jason (28)	5	91
SF	3	37
Brian (26)	6	90
SF	2	36

Match Play:

returns to
ALL SQUARE

Jason responds well to the growing competitive pressure. A perfectly played, temptation-resisting performance. All shots in position. Narrowly misses the par putt and has a tap-in to win the hole. Phil's pep talks continue apace with a long string of idioms!

Hole 18

Snatching Victory from the Jaws of Defeat?

To understand why at the end of this chapter Phil and I are hugging[103] you need some context. Firstly, in our series of match-play rounds against Brian and Jason we have not recently had a good run. It has been several weeks since we last avoided defeat and even longer since we won. Secondly, as a retirement present Phil paid for me to have a golf lesson.[104] I used the lesson to learn about chipping – my perennial weakness.

As we stand on the 18th tee the match-play situation is tense. Jason had taken hole 17 bringing the match to all square. The 18th is 147 yards from the yellow tees with a 120-yard carry over a lake with a playing fountain (which is only occasionally turned on – it is today – a sign perhaps?).

The banter is at an elevated level with various comments regarding "early baths" and the need for "balls that float". All expecting, as is usual for us, that somebody will drop their shot in the water. Phil the hydrophobia sufferer (see hole 10) is badly affected by this and the marshmallow begins to tremble.

Jason and Brian have the honour. Both hit good shots and reach the green. Both on the left though. Those evil white-cat-stroking men have positioned the hole over on the right. As always in the wrong position (reference my

---

103. Hugging but not kissing. As Phil is a Yorkshire man and Yorkshire men don't go in for such things. And from my point of view, he is wearing his marshmallow outfit which you really would not want to be seen kissing.
104. I know a lesser man could have been offended, but I thought it was a fabulous and thoughtful present.

rant on hole 16). However, with both Jason and Brian in good position (and more importantly dry) the pressure is on.

Phil goes first. He notes the trees overhanging the lake on the right so he decides to position his tee a couple of feet back from the markers so he can get a trajectory as far away from the trees as possible. This results in his teeing-off directly behind the chamfered marker. He strikes the ball. Dreadful stroke. The ball must have hit the angled chamfer on the tee marker because we witness the ball flying backwards and extremely close to Phil's head (I am sure if he had hair, it would have been parted). It drops on the bank to the lake and slowly and apologetically rolls in. Drop zone (DZ on map) for Phil.[105]

Our chances of winning are now in the serious deep stuff! I take my trusty 5-iron. Reciting a little Shakespeare: *"And gentlemen in England now a-bed shall think themselves accurs'd they were not here."*[106] With that patriotic hope in my heart I strike. It is a good connection, but the trajectory is all wrong. It is forward but not up. It is flying, laser like, for the lake. That seems to be that, I will be joining Phil in the drop zone. All hope of us avoiding defeat extinguished. But wait! The ball hits the water and bounces Barns Wallace-like[107] and makes it to dry land. Not the green but at least not sunk. Perhaps a glimmer of hope.

Phil plays a nice stroke from the drop zone and is on the green (he eventually gets down in 5). Then it is my shot.

---

105. I guess if anybody has bothered reading this far, they will know something about golf (and have concluded I know "not a lot"). However, just in case there is a non-golfer reading this then to explain the "Drop Zone". It is an area of shame where, when you have failed the big-boy shot, you are given another go from somewhere a little closer but at the cost of a stroke. In the case of hole 18 at Trent Lock it is on the left-hand side of the lake, just in front of the red markers (see map).
106. St Crispen Day speech made by King Henry V before the battle of Agincourt. *Henry V*, Act IV Scene iii (3) 18–67.
107. Inventor of the Bouncing Bomb.

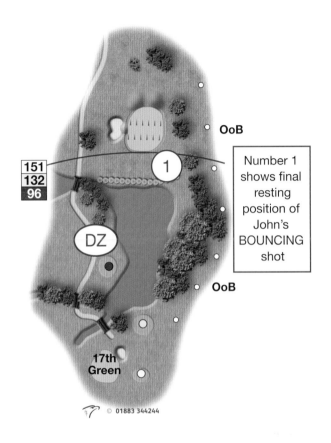

The ball is lying in the longer grass to the front right of the green. I remember the advice from my single golf lesson. Taking my sand-wedge, I keep my legs close together and open my stance out. I have a few practice swings (the coach seemed to think they helped). Then went for it. The shot felt perfect – like an eloquent sentence leaving my mouth. The ball floated up with seemingly effortless ease. It fell softly on the green and rolled slowly in a right-to-left curve getting ever closer to the hole. "It couldn't, could it?" shouts Phil. IT DID! For once the hole was in the correct position. All four of us cheer. Phil and I enjoy the aforementioned hug. "Best £25 I ever spent," he said.[108]

Jason and Brian both fail with their long putts and finish with a 4.

I start singing the Rend Collective song "Resurrection Day". Phil and Brian are a little more traditional and go for "Up From the Grave".

It seemed we were down and out before that ball leapt, salmon-like, off the lake. It must have seemed glum to the disciples of Jesus on the first Good Friday. They were "down and out". He had died that dreadful death on the cross and dying with him, it seemed, all the hopes of humanity. Had darkness prevailed over light, evil over good and death over life? Then the resounding resurrection answer:

Death has been swallowed up in victory
Where, O death is your victory?
Where, O death, is your sting?"[109]

The resurrection is one of "the", if not "the", best attested facts from ancient history. Go and read the now classic book *Who Moved the Stone?* by Frank Morison. An atheist who set out to prove the nonsense of the resurrection claim but as he reviewed the evidence his view and his life was changed.

Because Jesus rose there is hope, there is joy and there is life. Praise and thanks to him.

After finishing our various tuneful (not) renditions we all shake hands and congratulate one another. Brian has the lowest stroke score – so he has won. Jason has the highest

---

108. Until that moment I was unaware how much the lesson had cost. Very generous, thanks again, Phil!
109. 1 Corinthians 15:54-55.

Stableford score – so he has won. Phil and I won the match-play – so we have won. Again, I think, "You couldn't write it!" Everyone's a winner.[110] With another song on our lips, we head for the clubhouse and the well-earned breakfast cob.

To finish, though, a tantalising question. Did Jesus snatch victory from the jaws of defeat or was the cross the amazing, mysterious, wonderful, incredible plan all along?

The bridge of triumph or disaster depending on if you are heading for the 18th green or the drop zone.

---

110. Apologies to Hot Chocolate.

	Hole 18	Total
Par	3	
SI	13	
Phil (26)	5	96
SF	1	36
John (28)	2	97
SF	4	37
Jason (28)	4	95
SF	2	39
Brian (26)	4	94
SF	2	38

Match Play:

Phil and John
WIN by 1

A fantastic morning out with the clubs and friends. Can't wait for the next time!

Hope in Times of Fear **by Timothy Keller** (published by John Murray Press). Discussing the resurrection and the meaning of Easter.

In the Clubhouse

The round is done, and the Fellowship of the "Fore" requires refreshment and sustenance. We clean down the trolleys and golf bags and pack them into our cars. Then we remove tees, pencils, pitch-mark repairers, ball markers and spare balls from our pockets. Once we've changed shoes, visited the proper toilet, washed hands and checked our appearance in the mirror we are ready to enter the clubhouse. Not quite the rigmarole the high priest had to go through to get into the Holy of Holies in the temple[111] but still it always seems to take a while when in desperate need of a drink.

Trent Lock's clubhouse is a friendly place, lots of aimless but amenable chatter. Everyone seems relaxed and glad to be there. There are no cryptic or mysterious rules or rights of entry. You don't even need to play or have a sympathy with golf. It is a bar and restaurant and fully open to the public (and serves some great grub!). It is also becoming a popular business conference and wedding venue.

On this day there is a well-dressed group of five sitting round one of the tables. They are poring over glossy brochures and engaged in intense conversation. My Sherlock-like deductive powers lead me to conclude this is a bride-and-groom-to-be, with one set of parents, discussing wedding arrangements with a member of staff. I was not entirely sure that a bunch of noisy middle-aged (not to say "old") golfers descending into their space would help sell the place.

---

111. Leviticus 16:2-34.

During my career I travelled a lot and visited many venues. Some had strange etiquette and entrance requirements. Due to many hours on planes, I acquired various colours of executive cards that allowed me access into airports' luxury lounges. Never as friendly as Trent Lock's clubhouse – and entry was restricted and only a few were allowed in. Once when travelling alone I was entering such a lounge when next to me another lone traveller (looking very weary) was declined entry. I showed my gold card and asked if the tired traveller could be my guest. I cannot report, other than a grateful "thank you", that I had any other conversation with the man or struck up a lifelong friendship; I didn't. My point though – he was allowed in because of me.

When this life is done, the Bible is clear that there is heaven. A place where we can enjoy the presence of God forever. To enter, well, we can enter because of him. I love the passage in Hebrews 10 where it talks about Jesus sitting down at the right hand of God. The picture is one of completeness. He sits down because the task is complete. He has finished the round and can take his place in the clubhouse. The comparison the writer to the Hebrews makes is between Jesus ("this priest" verse 12) and the Hebrew priests who were not allowed to sit down. Why could they not sit down? Well, because their round is never complete. Sin has never been dealt with by the endless animal sacrifices (verse 11). The passage goes on to tell us about forgiveness (verse 17), about the new covenant (verse 16), about the Lordship of Christ (verse 13) and the right to enter into the presence of God (verse 19).

To compare the clubhouse with heaven is not a good illustration and not my purpose here. There is one point of comparison, though, and that is of fellowship. We will be in perfect fellowship with God and with each other, forever and forever.

Our standard fellowship-enhancing fare after 18 holes is a sausage or bacon cob. If we are feeling extravagant, we ask for an egg to be added. All washed down with a large pot of tea. On this day the waiter brings out the cobs and approaches from behind, invisible to Jason. Jason, at that very moment, tries to swat a fly away. It is an air shot. He misses the fly but his follow through connects cleanly with a sausage and egg cob on the waiter's tray. Jason's cleanest strike of the day! It is one of those moments where things seem to move in slow motion. The spinning cob, spraying grease and yoke, is heading in the direction of the well-dressed "bride-to-be" sitting opposite. As one we shout, "fore right".[112] So, the round ends as it began with the Fellowship of the "Fore" together and in full voice.

If you have read this far, then thank you. I hope you have enjoyed it, and may God continue to bless you and grant you many more rounds.

Can I suggest **All About Heaven by David Oliver** (Malcolm Down Publishing)? Through a thorough examination of the relevant biblical texts, David provides a thrilling view of the future.

---

112. Sadly, the bride-to-be clearly was not a golfer. On hearing the shout "fore" she looked up rather than ducking down and, as a result, took the sausage and egg cob full in the face!

The Scorecard

Just in case you are interested.

	Hole 1	Hole 2	Hole 3	Hole 4	Hole 5	Hole 6	Hole 7	Hole 8	Hole 9	Out
Par	5	4	3	4	4	3	4	4	3	
SI	10	8	16	2	14	12	4	6	18	
Phil (26)	7	6	4	5	4	4	6	4	5	45
SF	1	2	2	3	3	2	2	4	1	20
John (28)	8	5	4	6	5	5	4	6	5	48
SF	1	3	2	2	2	1	4	2	1	18
Jason (28)	8	6	4	5	4	3	6	6	4	46
SF	1	2	2	3	3	3	4	2	2	20
Brian (26)	8	5	4	4	5	4	7	6	2	45
SF	0	3	2	4	2	2	1	2	4	20

	Hole 10	Hole 11	Hole 12	Hole 13	Hole 14	Hole 15	Hole 16	Hole 17	Hole 18	Total
Par	4	4	3	4	4	5	5	4	3	
SI	7	17	11	1	5	15	9	3	13	
Phil (26)	8	5	4	3	5	6	8	6	5	95
SF	0	2	2	5	3	1	0	2	2	37
John (28)	6	6	6	4	6	6	6	7	2	97
SF	2	1	0	4	2	2	3	1	4	37
Jason (28)	7	5	4	5	5	7	7	5	4	95
SF	1	2	2	3	3	1	2	3	2	39
Brian (26)	7	5	4	6	5	5	7	6	4	94
SF	1	2	2	2	3	3	1	2	2	38

Missing the Cut

I had a number of ideas that I took out of the final version of the round. Many were rubbish but some I, kind of, liked – so have included here.

Hole 2 – Rules of the Game

I considered debating the formulation of the rules of golf. How did they come about? I know that the recent and updated compilation was through a working group comprising people from both sides of the Atlantic (the R&A and the USGA). Presumably, though, in days gone by, before the level of global communication/collaboration we have today, there would have been many variations on the basic game. Who decided what was right and what was wrong? This is a very interesting debate if applied to ethics and morality. The basic rules of life. Without a view of a transcendent God or overarching human ethic, who decides what is wrong or right? The rules of life can become a matter of current taste and not cogent truth. Watching society, it is not difficult to imagine a game of golf and the ensuing chaos when everyone believes they have the authority to make their own rules. Perhaps many a 7-iron wrapped around many a neck would be the result? Yet the direction of modern culture and the internalisation of ethics is driving us in that very direction. "If it feels right – then do it." Imagine – no common set of principles to follow and no ultimately good authority to refer to. Imagine the community of humanity refusing to agree on any principles by which to live and each individual's perception ruling in that singular instance of humanity. At this point (you can tell) I am getting seriously out of my philosophical depth, hence I am not attempting to take it any further. However, if you want to read more on that subject then can I point you to part 1 of Dr Carl R. Trueman's book, *The Rise and Triumph of the Modern Self*.[113] As I have already noted, it is a shame that Carl does not play golf; I am sure he could have drawn some useful illustrations from the game. His loss for sure!

Hole 8 – Lost and Found

Many years ago, I visited a local 9-hole course with my young (I guess around 7-year-old) son Isaac. The course was short and a little ragged around the edges (that was 21-year-old Isaac's description of this book when I asked him to read over a few chapters!). Isaac was not playing; he had agreed to be my caddie for the round. He soon got bored and derived much more fun from looking for lost balls in the rough, bushes and trees. A young version of Phil, but not dressed in a marshmallow outfit. He borrowed my 5-iron as a scavenging tool. He returned to me with pockets, hat and hands all full of balls (even the odd Callaway) but no club. The club was lost to me. Isaac was apologetic and a little surprised at my sanguine acceptance of the loss. I pointed out that the club often misbehaved and probably deserved its fate!

Hole 10 – From There to Here

While discussing preaching I asked Phil if he had listened to my latest effort on YouTube. He said he had, but at 40 minutes it was far too long.[114] He reminded me of an old lady by the name of Miss Morley whose advice to all

---

113.   Dr Carl R. Trueman, *The Rise and Triumph of the Modern Self* (Crossway Books, 2020).
114.   I did comment that YouTube has a pause button. He did not need to listen to it all in one go!

people that preach was brief but worth repeating: "Stand up, speak up, shut up."

Hole 10 – From There to Here

Phil asked me to ensure I mentioned that on one occasion he chipped over the lake and into the hole! Thereby managing a par after his second hit the water. This did not fit with the narrative of this round so it missed the cut, but I assure you, it did happen ... once!

Hole 14 – I Talk to the Wind (the necessity of prayer)

On Mondays I play with Phil, Simon and Steve. We usually pair up as Phil and Simon versus Steve and me. Tee-off is generally 9am. At 7am Steve and I are just waking up, Simon (so he tells us) is on the driving range and Phil (so he tells us) is in a prayer meeting. He always remembers to pray for Simon on the range, hoping that Simon's extended practice will prove to be useful in the subsequent match. The moral of this – our prayers should be far more God and others focused than selfish. Hmmm . . . Phil is partnering Simon so there is a selfish element to that. You can see now why this missed the cut.

Hole 16 – Complaints to the Hon-Sec

An alternative version: To us incapable golfers this is the most difficult hole on the course. If you manage to go straight it has 3 separate and lateral water hazards. The first shot requires a carry of over 170 yards, dropping the ball onto a peninsular. Almost impossible for us.

The four of us stand on the tee looking at the imposing challenge, steeling ourselves for the pending ordeal. I pass the whiskey round again and off we go.

Remarkably Jason hits the peninsular. Flushed with his success he visualises smacking his second within pitching distance of the green (this is only possible in Jason's imagination). The swing is mighty and the connection is good but in the wrong place on the ball. We all look heavenwards but cannot see the ball; in fact, the ball has not left the ground. It has been driven a good few inches down into the soft earth. After a short debate we conclude a free drop (after digging the ball out) is probably the kinder option to the fairway versus the possibility of the major excavation that Jason's next shot will incur.

Reflection: Do we sometimes get too fixed on our way? We can see how we want things to be done. We pursue this with all the power and purpose of Jason's swing but somehow, we get the connection wrong. We end up hurting others and ourselves and not moving things on in the way that we would want.

Peter had some very clear views of who Jesus was and what he was to do. He swung and got the connection wrong.[115] We need to constantly check, by persistent prayer, reading the Bible, following the Spirit's guidance, that we are on the right fairway!

Hole 19 – In the Clubhouse

If John Newton were a golfer, I am sure the last verse of his famous "Amazing Grace" hymn would read:

When we've been round ten thousand times
Straight driving, chip and run
We've no less days to hit fairways
Than when we first begun

---

115. Mark 8:31-33.

Acknowledgements

There are a number of people who deserve a mention and a vote of thanks. So, in no particular order:

- Eddie and the staff and members of Trent Lock Golf and Country Club. Without you guys there would be nowhere to play! A special "shout out" to Sharron who put up with my constant pestering emails.

- Malcolm, my publisher, and all from Malcolm Down Publishing Ltd. Without Malcolm this book would have got stuck in the rough on the first fairway. Malcolm understands this book, being an incompetent golfer himself.

- Louise for editing, correcting my constant misuse of CAPITAL letters and for declaring the book to be "fun".

- To my golfing buddies, the Fellowship of the "Fore" and all the other friends who join us in club-swinging, fairway-hacking and green-missing. Without you it really would be no fun at all.

- To Carl, Rico, Ray and Jason for their kind comments. It was an encouragement that busy people took time out to read what I had written. Commitment above and beyond!

- Pauline, Matt, Lydia and Isaac for being the most wonderful family I could ever imagine. I am truly blessed. A particular thank you to Lydia for encouraging me, proof-reading and adding some creative content (probably the good bits). She is in the process of writing the Merit-Hunters Series. If you are a man of a "certain age" you may have children in Generation Y. If so, they will love the Merit-Hunters Series, so there is my recommendation for the next birthday or Christmas present you need to buy. Just search online for L.G. Jenkins.

- Above all, thank you to God my Father for all things, including the great game of golf and the glorious gospel of Jesus Christ.

The Author

John Horry recently retired from an all-consuming senior role in a multi-national healthcare organisation. He has now turned his attention to more leisurely pursuits including working on his golf handicap, so far without much success. For many years John has been part of the leadership team at SBC (Stapleford Baptist Church), a church located in a small-town west of Nottingham. In that role he is engaged in a teaching ministry regularly speaking and leading meetings. *The Gospel in Golf* is his first (and probably only) attempt at writing.

As Carl R. Trueman says in his foreword, John recognises that he "married up" – to Pauline. They have three grown children: Matt, Lydia and Isaac.

Final Putt

I really hope you have found this a useful and fun read. If you would like to contact me or share any of your amusing golfing anecdotes or your reflections on life inspired by events on a golf course then please join me and a growing fellowship of incompetent golfers at:

www.gospelingolf.com